How to Pass
Advanced
Verbal
Reasoning Tests

More titles in the Testing series:

The Advanced Numeracy Test Workbook	978 0 7494 6226 0
Aptitude, Personality and Motivation Tests	978 0 7494 5651 1
The Brain Fitness Workout	978 0 7494 5982 6
The Complete Personality Assessment	978 0 7494 6373 1
The Graduate Psychometric Test Workbook	978 0 7494 6174 4
How to Master Psychometric Tests	978 0 7494 6128 7
How to Pass Advanced Aptitude Tests	978 0 7494 6142 3
How to Pass Advanced Numeracy Tests	978 0 7494 6789 0
How to Pass Advanced Verbal Reasoning Tests	978 0 7494 6793 7
How to Pass Data Interpretation Tests	978 0 7494 6232 1
How to Pass Diagrammatic Reasoning Tests	978 0 7494 4971 1
How to Pass Graduate Psychometric Tests	978 0 7494 6799 9
How to Pass the Life in the UK Test	978 0 7494 5723 5
How to Pass Numeracy Tests	978 0 7494 6791 3
How to Pass Numerical Reasoning Tests	978 0 7494 6797 5
How to Pass the Police Selection System	978 0 7494 5712 9
How to Pass Professional Level Psychometric Tests	978 0 7494 6795 1
How to Pass the QTS Numeracy and Literacy Skills Tests	978 0 7494 6241 3
How to Pass Selection Tests	978 0 7494 6211 6
How to Pass the UK's National Firefighter Selection Process	978 0 7494 6205 5
How to Pass Verbal Reasoning Tests	978 0 7494 5696 2
How to Succeed at an Assessment Centre	978 0 7494 6229 1
IQ and Aptitude Tests	978 0 7494 6195 9
IQ and Psychometric Tests	978 0 7494 6196 6
IQ and Psychometric Test Workbook	978 0 7494 6261 1
Management Level Psychometric Assessments	978 0 7494 5691 7
Test and Assess Your Brain Quotient	978 0 7494 5416 6
Test Your Emotional Intelligence	978 0 7494 6230 7
Test Your EQ	978 0 7494 5535 4

www.koganpage.com

You are reading one of the thousands of books
published by **Kogan Page**. As Europe's leading
independent business book publishers **Kogan Page**
has always sought to provide up-to-the-minute books
that offer practical guidance at affordable prices.

KoganPage

How to Pass
Advanced
Verbal
Reasoning Tests

Essential practice for English usage,
critical reasoning and reading
comprehension tests

Mike Bryon
Second edition

KoganPage

LONDON PHILADELPHIA NEW DELHI

Publisher's note

Every possible effort has been made to ensure that the information contained in this book is accurate at the time of going to press, and the publishers and authors cannot accept responsibility for any errors or omissions, however caused. No responsibility for loss or damage occasioned to any person acting, or refraining from action, as a result of the material in this publication can be accepted by the editor, the publisher or any of the authors.

First published in Great Britain in 2008 by Kogan Page Limited
Second edition 2010
Reissued 2013

120 Pentonville Road
London N1 9JN
United Kingdom
www.koganpage.com

1518 Walnut Street, Suite 1100
Philadelphia PA 19102
USA

4737/23 Ansari Road
Daryaganj
New Delhi 110002
India

ISBN   978 0 7494 6793 7
E-ISBN   978 0 7494 6794 4

British Library Cataloguing-in-Publication Data

A CIP record for this book is available from the British Library.

Library of Congress Cataloging-in-Publication Data

Library of Congress Control Number: 2012051522

Typeset by Graphicraft Limited, Hong Kong
Printed and bound in India by Replika Press Pvt Ltd

Contents

Preface vii

Mike Bryon – A pioneer in test coaching ix

1 Verbal reasoning tests 1

For some candidates, verbal tests are their
   worst nightmare 2

If English is not your first language 3

If you are dyslexic or suffer some other disability 3

Tests that hide in a bundle of forms! 4

Personality questionnaires 5

If you are invited to an assessment centre 21

An example of what such a day might include 24

The group exercise or role play 25

Presentations 29

Written exercises 32

2 The winning approach 36

3 110 Warm-up questions 42

Tests of verbal ability 42

Word link: opposites 43

Word link: synonyms 46

Find the new word 47

Word swap 50

Sentence sequence 55

4   100 English usage questions 66

Correctly complete the sentence 67
Identify the correct sentence 77

5   100 True, false or cannot tell questions 97

6   Decision analysis 130

Decision analysis questions 131

7   Four timed realistic tests with interpretations of your score 147

Test 1. Sentence sequence 148
Test 2. Word swap 164
Test 3. English usage 171
Test 4. Reading comprehension and critical reasoning 182
An interpretation of your score in the practice tests 195

8   Answers and detailed explanations 198

Chapter 1. Personality questionnaire 198
Chapter 3. 110 Warm-up questions 205
Chapter 4. 100 English usage questions 208
Chapter 5. 100 True, false or cannot tell questions 216
Chapter 6. Decision analysis 227
Chapter 7. Four timed realistic tests with interpretations
     of your score 234

Preface

Stand out from the crowd

If you have been searching for help to prepare for a verbal reasoning test at the advanced level then you have found it. This book has been especially written for the candidate facing an advanced level test and it contains hundreds of questions, in fact over 500. If you are applying for graduate or managerial jobs, for example in finance-related graduate jobs, the NHS Graduate Training Scheme or the Big Four accounting firms, banks or consultancies, then you will face a battery of sub-tests including an advanced verbal reasoning test. This book reflects the difficulty of these tests, and the practice questions will help ensure that you improve your score and chances of a pass.

Use this book to stand out from the crowd of other applicants. Before you sit an advanced verbal reasoning test be sure to work through these practice questions and tests. Score them and go through the explanations of any questions that you got wrong. Finally, read the interpretation of your score and amend your programme of revision accordingly. You will find lots more questions at all levels in other books in the Kogan Page testing list. If you have difficulties in locating sufficient practice questions of a particular sort then by all means contact me at help@mikebryon.com and I will be happy to provide you with details of any that I know.

This book offers unbeatable practice for tests online or administered with pen and paper or at an assessment centre. You will find lots of advice, insight and tips on all the major types of advanced verbal reasoning tests in use today, including written exercises, group exercises, role plays and presentations. Use it and very soon you will be much faster at answering these questions and achieving a much higher score. It is ideal for the candidate who wants to prepare systematically for a psychometric test of advanced verbal reasoning skills – and pass.

Mike Bryon – A pioneer in test coaching

Employers used to argue that candidates could not improve their score in psychometric tests. Mike Bryon proved otherwise. It is now unanimously acknowledged that every candidate can improve how they perform in these common selection tools.

Mike Bryon was first published in 1991 and now has 17 books in print on how to pass the tests and assessments used by large employers. He is the best selling author on the subject. Each book contains advice on the winning mindset, insights and tips, hundreds of realistic example questions, practice tests, answers, explanations and interpretations of your score. Hundreds of thousands of people have used the books to get down to some serious score improving practice and succeed in the test and assessments they face. The books have sold worldwide and have been translated into many foreign languages including Indonesian, Portuguese, Russian, Polish, Indian and Chinese.

After three years of postgraduate research into adult learning at the University of Birmingham (UK) he founded a consultancy, and for 15 years he provided recruitment and diversity consultancy to organisations in every industrial sector and a great many major UK and international companies, including departments of the UK Government, national utilities, high street retail chains, rail companies, local and emergency authorities, and multinationals such as the Ford Motor Company and British Airport Authorities. The consultancy contributed extensively to EU research programmes with research partners drawn from across the union.

His books review the strategies and provide the practice you need to gain a competitive advantage. Importantly they offer practice at a level that reflects that of the actual tests. These books really do offer hundreds of realistic practice questions; 400 or 500 as a minimum. Many of the titles offer far more than this. *The Ultimate Psychometric Test Book* contains over 1,000 practice questions and is perfect for the candidate who faces tests at the intermediate level or seeks an introduction to graduate material.

The titles reach across the whole testing spectrum from inter-mediate through to graduate and the high flyer. There is winning advice, insights and tips on personality questionnaires, situational awareness tests, assessment days, group exercises, role plays and in-tray or e-tray exercises. There are books to help candidates who dare to dream of a single career goal including applicant firefighters, candidates for the UK civil service (including the FastStream), post-graduate business schools applicants who face the GMAT and medical school applicants who face the UKCAT. Mike Bryon has also written on secondary transfer for children of 11 years of age, and adults who face a test as speakers of English as a second language.

Mike Bryon has over 10 years of experience in the training room, making sure every candidate demonstrates their full potential and realises the career of their choice. His groundbreaking approach has proved decisive for countless thousands of candidates.

His work remains contemporary through his continual research and writing and through the many readers who contact him for advice and suggestions on sources of practice questions. During your programme of review, if you hit a problem or if you would like suggestions of sources of practice material then e-mail Mike Bryon at: help@mikebryon.com.

Chapter 1
Verbal reasoning tests

At some stage of your career you are certain to face a verbal reasoning psychometric test. This can involve multiple-choice tests of your work-related verbal abilities organized as tests of your command of English usage, reading comprehension, written assignments, group discussions or presentations. If you are a graduate or applicant to managerial positions or postgraduate courses you are very likely to face a psychometric test of your advanced verbal skills.

Beyond the first stage of a recruitment process your qualifications count for little. Once employers have established that you have satisfied the formal requirements for the position they then turn to investigate your abilities in a range of other competencies relevant to the position; these are bound to include your verbal reasoning skills.

Psychometric tests of verbal reasoning are not like blood tests, rolling up your sleeve and putting up with the discomfort of the needle. They are only indicators of potential and you (the subject) have considerable influence over the outcome. This is good news because you can learn to do really well in them and, through preparation, can pass something you might otherwise have failed.

Psychometric tests of verbal reasoning skills come in many forms, at different stages of your career and at different stages of the recruitment process. Below are descriptions of the more common types. Look out for them, use the advice, insight and practice material provided here and you will maximize your chances of success.

In preparation for any verbal test it is still advisable to revise the rules of grammar and punctuation. Be aware that many tests are used worldwide and for this reason they may follow either US or English practice with regard to spelling and punctuation. It is very unlikely that the test will score against either convention, so feel free to follow whichever you grew up using or were taught. It would be a bad test that asked you to identify the correct spelling in the case of, for example, color (US spelling) and colour (UK spelling).

Something you may have to get used to is the lack of certainty found in verbal reasoning tests relative to numerical questions. In maths there is a right answer and little room for argument. But verbal tests are less definite because they are often concerned with judgement, inference and context, which, at the advanced level, can require the drawing of some fine distinctions. It is not usual for candidates to feel that the answer they selected is at least as correct as the given answer. If you ever find yourself in this situation then the likelihood is that you have to work to bring your judgement more into line with the question setter. When a test author is designing high-level verbal tests he or she has to draw these very fine distinctions between the suggested answers; much finer distinctions than we draw in normal English usage. Practice will help you learn to answer the questions according to the judge's view of what is right – and remember, the judge's decision is final.

For some candidates, verbal tests are their worst nightmare

It is common to come across otherwise accomplished candidates who find verbal tests a real challenge. These individuals may have undertaken a great deal of technical training and may score very highly in numerical or non-verbal sub-tests, but do far less well in verbal tests. Organizations are looking for good scores in all the tests they set and don't offset a good score in one for a bad score in another. So if you are such a candidate and up to now have accomplished a great deal without verbal reasoning skills commensurate with the rest of your abilities, now is the time to put the situation to rights and get down to some serious score-improving practice.

At the advanced level a common type of verbal test involves a series of paragraphs and you having to answer questions about each. These questions are foremost about making judgements where you have to answer true, false or cannot tell. Remember, verbal tests lack the certainty of numerical tests, so be sure to allow sufficient time for practice to bring your judgement into line with that of the question setter's. Avoid choosing the 'cannot tell' option too frequently. Practice will bring a big improvement to your score in verbal tests. Set aside the necessary time, get hold of sufficient practice questions, and you will go on to pass these common tests.

If English is not your first language

You are going to find parts of every verbal test in English a greater challenge, so adjust your programme of revision accordingly. Spend plenty of time reading quality newspapers and journals to build your vocabulary and improve your proficiency at assimilating the meanings of complex sentences. Look up unfamiliar words.

If you are dyslexic or suffer some other disability

Speak to the employer straightaway, provide full details of your condition and be clear on the special arrangements you require. You may be allowed extra time, or be provided with a test reader or someone to record your answers. Braille or large text versions of the test may be made available. It is reasonable to expect that your requirements are given proper consideration and wherever possible are accommodated. Evidence of your condition may be required.

Tests that hide in a bundle of forms!

Verbal reasoning tests are always being changed and novel assessments trialled and introduced. A few years ago, for example, a verbal test was most likely to include questions that asked you to identify synonyms and antonyms, or tested your spelling or command of the rules of English grammar. These styles of question are still used but are becoming less common. Contemporary tests are more likely to comprise a passage of information and a series of questions relating to it, to which you have to answer true, false or cannot tell. Written assignments, memos or work-related exercises are also increasingly common. Nowadays you are also very likely to have to complete a personality questionnaire.

Every organization requires you to complete a bundle of forms on paper or online. To begin with make sure your application and/or CV are error free. Many organizations will reject your application out of hand if they find errors. You will not believe the number of candidates rejected at this early stage for this easily avoidable reason. Very often the forms you are required to complete include some type of self-assessment – these are psychometric tests and to some extent they are verbal reasoning tests. Most candidates give them far too little thought. This is a mistake as they may well be the basis of selection at the stage when the largest numbers of applicants are rejected. Look out for them – they comprise a series of questions to which you must indicate your preference. For example:

Good leadership is about boldness far more than listening skills.

agree   *neither agree nor disagree*   *disagree*

Your answers should depend on the organization to which you are applying and the sort of person it is looking for. Always keep the job role and organization at the forefront of your mind. Answer with care questions which, for example, imply a disregard for health and safety or behaviour that amounts to physical aggression or gross misconduct.

Personality questionnaires

The aim of such self assessments is to expand the range of infor-mation available on candidates by providing a report on attributes and characteristics regarding the candidate's personal style or how they might act at work if employed. Take this to mean that they will use your responses to build a psychometric profile of your attitude and personality. While people may be reluctant to call them tests and they say no answer is right or wrong, your answers may be used to decide if your application should be accepted or rejected – so take the questions seriously.

Some people mistakenly believe that you cannot improve your performance in this style of test. They are wrong, because many people rush this type of exercise and do not give the statements it comprises sufficient consideration.

It is essential in this type of exercise that you answer the ques-tions truthfully, but it is equally essential that you keep the context of the question at the front of your mind. With each question, ask yourself: 'If I worked for this company how would I respond in that situation?' Take the first example of the practice questions below: 'I would describe myself as tactful.' You should be able to answer this question positively. When you are out with your friends or at home with your family you might not always act tactfully but this would be the totally wrong response in the context of the question. How you sometimes act with your friends or family is irrelevant. In the vast majority of jobs tact is essential and candidates who cannot describe themselves as tactful may not be selected.

Responding truthfully to the questions will sometimes mean that you admit to something that risks counting against you. For example, if you have not undertaken voluntary work and you are asked if you have, be prepared to say so. It is unlikely that a few negative-scoring answers will significantly affect your overall score – and anyway, if you lie and it is discovered at a later stage your application may be rejected.

Look out and take extra care if any questions include double negatives. They can be very misleading, and you can easily answer them in a way that you did not intend. An example of this sort of question might be: 'Do you agree or disagree with the statement: It is not true that I'm 18 years of age.' This sort of question can be confusing, especially if you are suffering anxiety during the real test. The way to approach this sort of question is to break it down into parts. Begin by answering the factual bit of the question, in this instance 'are you 18 years of age'. Now add the 'it is not true' part of the question. This in effect changes your answer. If you are 18 then you would disagree that it is not true that you are 18 years of age.

When answering the questions it is best not to give too many responses that imply strongly held views. If you do, you might risk the impression that you are someone too strident in your opinions, with too many strongly held views. It is also best not to give too many non-committal responses either, as this might indicate that you find it difficult to make your mind up or commit yourself. It is fine to give some of these strongly held or non-committal responses, but try not to indicate too many.

Be sure that you are confident recognizing the synonyms of key personality attributes desirable in the role to which you are applying. You need to be familiar with the synonyms so that you can confidently agree with or disagree with a statement that describes an attribute as desirable in the role.

It is important to be consistent in your response. These tests often return to investigate the same issue a number of times (each may be worded differently). You should try to answer these related questions consistently. It can be a bit tricky because these related questions are spread out through the body of questions.

Some questions require you to read additional information before you respond to a series of questions that follow. This style of question is sometimes called a situational awareness questionnaire; you should answer the questions only in the context of the information contained in the situation.

Below you will find 50 practice questions, some of which involve a situation. In most cases you have to decide if you agree or disagree or strongly agree or strongly disagree. Because your answer will depend on your and the organization's preferred style of working, it is not possible to give right answers to these questions. In the answers chapter, however, I have indicated what is likely to be inferred from each question.

A sample personality questionnaire

Q1   I would describe myself as tactful.

Strongly agree
Agree
Cannot agree or disagree
Disagree
Strongly disagree

Answer [   ]

Q2   A nice customer can expect the same level of service as one who is rude.

Strongly agree
Agree
Cannot agree or disagree
Disagree
Strongly disagree

Answer [   ]

Q3   I have a very good written style.

Strongly agree
Agree
Cannot agree or disagree
Disagree
Strongly disagree

Answer [   ]

Q4   If I was asked to do something that was not in my job description I would politely explain to my line manager that I would do it this time but could he or she arrange for someone else to help in future.

Strongly agree
Agree
Cannot agree or disagree
Disagree
Strongly disagree

Answer [   ]

Q5   I find intolerance intolerable.

Strongly agree
Agree
Cannot agree or disagree
Disagree
Strongly disagree

Answer [   ]

Q6   If I drink alcohol in the privacy of my own home then it is none of my employer's business.

Strongly agree
Agree
Cannot agree or disagree
Disagree
Strongly disagree

Answer [   ]

Q7   The more matter-of-fact a suggestion the more I prefer it.

Strongly agree
Agree
Cannot agree or disagree
Disagree
Strongly disagree

Answer [   ]

Q8   Leadership is more to do with leading people through the unforeseen than predicting the future and preparing for it.

Strongly agree
Agree
Cannot agree or disagree
Disagree
Strongly disagree

Answer [ ]

Q9   Playing the occasional practical joke on a colleague at work is not OK.

Strongly agree
Agree
Cannot agree or disagree
Disagree
Strongly disagree

Answer [ ]

Q10   I like to work in traditional ways.

Strongly agree
Agree
Cannot agree or disagree
Disagree
Strongly disagree

Answer [ ]

Q11   I would hesitate before I rang a colleague to discuss a work-related issue outside working hours.

Strongly agree
Agree
Cannot agree or disagree
Disagree
Strongly disagree

Answer [ ]

Q12 I have a very direct approach.

Strongly agree
Agree
Cannot agree or disagree
Disagree
Strongly disagree

Answer [   ]

Q13 I would not challenge the status quo.

Strongly agree
Agree
Cannot agree or disagree
Disagree
Strongly disagree

Answer [   ]

Q14 I let bygones be bygones.

Strongly agree
Agree
Cannot agree or disagree
Disagree
Strongly disagree

Answer [   ]

Q15 I like repetitive work.

Strongly agree
Agree
Cannot agree or disagree
Disagree
Strongly disagree

Answer [   ]

Q16 Some less than perfect behaviour has to be expected because boys will be boys.

Strongly agree
Agree
Cannot agree or disagree
Disagree
Strongly disagree

Answer

Q17 My success to date is due to my ruthless drive and determination.

Strongly agree
Agree
Cannot agree or disagree
Disagree
Strongly disagree

Answer

Situation 1

Answer questions 18, 19 and 20 assuming that the following situation applied to you:

It is your job to record attendance and hand the paperwork into the management at the end of each day's work. It has been a very stressful Monday, and made the more stressful by the fact that Peter and Sarah are off work sick. Peter often calls in sick on Mondays but it is very unusual for Sarah not to be at work. Despite his sick record Peter is a very popular member of the team and John, another member of the team, knows Peter's family and he says that Peter has problems at home. The management have held a series of meetings with Peter and you know that he has had a number of warnings about his attendance. Despite the fact that you are two down, your team rallies around and gets the job done. However, everyone is pretty tired and tempers are a little frayed.

Q18 Which of the following actions would you take?

A. Ask John to speak to Peter's family and explain that Peter could well be sacked if he does not improve his attendance record.

B. Leave it to the management to resolve and submit accurate attendance records.

C. Submit records that show Sarah off sick but record Peter as having been at work when he was not.

D. Submit accurate attendance records but explain to management that you understand Peter has problems at home.

Answer [   ]

Q19 Under the circumstances it would be acceptable for members of the team to let off a little steam by using bad language as long as no customers hear them.

Strongly agree

Agree

Cannot agree or disagree

Disagree

Strongly disagree

Answer [   ]

Q20 The next time Peter was in work one of the team was being less than respectful towards him; while this was not the best thing to do it was excusable in the circumstances.

Strongly agree

Agree

Cannot agree or disagree

Disagree

Strongly disagree

Answer [   ]

Q21 I dislike regulations because they stifle creativity.

Strongly agree
Agree
Cannot agree or disagree
Disagree
Strongly disagree

Answer

Q22 What matters is the intrinsic quality of a thing or person.

Strongly agree
Agree
Cannot agree or disagree
Disagree
Strongly disagree

Answer

Q23 Harsh words hurt us because we let them and we should all toughen up a bit so they don't.

Strongly agree
Agree
Cannot agree or disagree
Disagree
Strongly disagree

Answer

Q24 Someone who has mismanaged their affairs is not best left to suffer the consequences.

Strongly agree
Agree
Cannot agree or disagree
Disagree
Strongly disagree

Answer

Q25 I tend to get stressed if things do not go to plan.

Strongly agree
Agree
Cannot agree or disagree
Disagree
Strongly disagree

Answer [   ]

Situation 2

Answer questions 26, 27 and 28 assuming that the following situation applied to you:

Big Bank is a very wealthy institution but has a reputation for paying the lowest salaries in the industry while expecting their staff to work extremely hard. You have worked there for many years and often come in early and work during your lunch break because otherwise you would not manage to complete all your tasks. Your manager often tells you that she can't pay you more for all this extra work, and that Big Bank does not deserve such a good worker. In fact she spends most of her time in her office making personal calls and e-mailing friends. She pays very little attention to what is going on in her department and if staff raise any issue of concern with her it seems that she takes no notice, as nothing ever changes.

Q26 I would feel uncomfortable if I knew that my manager's lack of attention meant that money was being wasted on unnecessary office equipment and stationery.

Strongly agree
Agree
Cannot agree or disagree
Disagree
Strongly disagree

Answer [   ]

Q27 If I thought that a colleague was making inappropriate remarks toward a new worker I would:

A. Leave it for them to resolve.

B. Report my concerns to the manager.

C. Tell the colleague that I thought the remarks were inappropriate and report my concerns to the manager.

D. Tell the new worker that there is no point reporting it as the manager will do nothing.

Answer [   ]

Q28 Given all the extra hours of work that I do it would be OK if I occasionally took a few pens and some paper home for my children.

Strongly agree

Agree

Cannot agree or disagree

Disagree

Strongly disagree

Answer [   ]

Q29 I would be surprised if I offered to shake someone's hand and they declined.

Strongly agree

Agree

Cannot agree or disagree

Disagree

Strongly disagree

Answer [   ]

Q30 Prudence is undervalued in many organizations.

Strongly agree

Agree

Cannot agree or disagree
Disagree
Strongly disagree

Answer [   ]

Q31   I work best with the minimum number of distractions.

Strongly agree
Agree
Cannot agree or disagree
Disagree
Strongly disagree

Answer [   ]

Q32   I do not get bothered very much if a job is slightly dangerous.

Strongly agree
Agree
Cannot agree or disagree
Disagree
Strongly disagree

Answer [   ]

Q33   There are some people who I just know I am not going to get on with.

Strongly agree
Agree
Cannot agree or disagree
Disagree
Strongly disagree

Answer [   ]

Q34   Various people say one thing but they sometimes mean something else.

Strongly agree
Agree
Cannot agree or disagree

Disagree
Strongly disagree

Answer

Q35 It is never necessary to lie.

Strongly agree
Agree
Cannot agree or disagree
Disagree
Strongly disagree

Answer

Q36 I would say it is almost never right to steal.

Strongly agree
Agree
Cannot agree or disagree
Disagree
Strongly disagree

Answer

Q37 Being strident in order to make an important point is not necessarily a bad thing.

Strongly agree
Agree
Cannot agree or disagree
Disagree
Strongly disagree

Answer

Q38 There is nothing new under the sun.

Strongly agree
Agree
Cannot agree or disagree
Disagree
Strongly disagree

Answer

Q39 I am uncomfortable with vagueness.

Strongly agree
Agree
Cannot agree or disagree
Disagree
Strongly disagree

Answer

Q40 I treat people the way I expect to be treated myself.

Strongly agree
Agree
Cannot agree or disagree
Disagree
Strongly disagree

Answer

Situation 3

Answer questions 41, 42 and 43 assuming that you want to work for the Right Corporation:

The Right Corporation was founded just two years ago and has enjoyed remarkable success. The founder puts this down to the strength of its business relationships, inclusive working style and the ability of its management team to visualize, communicate and deploy strategies. Above all else he believes you have to give staff the room and trust to do their job and ensure that they feel that they can succeed. He describes his own success as due to his ability to think laterally; what he describes as 'thinking outside the box'. He is now looking to add to the staff people who will help consolidate the success of the Corporation and expects this to involve the introduction of business parameters and more formal working procedures.

Q41 I am naturally averse to risk.

Strongly agree
Agree

Cannot agree or disagree
Disagree
Strongly disagree

Answer

Q42   Every business can benefit from a few policies and
rules but very soon they can be bad for business.

Strongly agree
Agree
Cannot agree or disagree
Disagree
Strongly disagree

Answer

Q43   I believe that those qualified in an area should make
the greatest contribution when the subject is being
debated.

Strongly agree
Agree
Cannot agree or disagree
Disagree
Strongly disagree

Answer

Q44   All's well that ends well.

Strongly agree
Agree
Cannot agree or disagree
Disagree
Strongly disagree

Answer

Q45 Right or wrong, the customer is always right.

Strongly agree
Agree
Cannot agree or disagree
Disagree
Strongly disagree

Answer

Q46 I would prefer to enter a competition as a part of a team than as an individual.

Strongly agree
Agree
Cannot agree or disagree
Disagree
Strongly disagree

Answer

Q47 I do not say one thing and do another.

Strongly agree
Agree
Cannot agree or disagree
Disagree
Strongly disagree

Answer

Q48 You can teach an old dog new tricks.

Strongly agree
Agree
Cannot agree or disagree
Disagree
Strongly disagree

Answer

Q49 If I could not complete my work because a light bulb had
blown then I would offer to change it.

Strongly agree
Agree
Cannot agree or disagree
Disagree
Strongly disagree

Answer

Q50 If I make a mistake I first put it right then I tell someone in
authority about it.

Strongly agree
Agree
Cannot agree or disagree
Disagree
Strongly disagree

Answer

End of questionnaire.

If you are invited to an assessment centre

Most usually employers use assessment centres to look at your
communication skills, interpersonal skills and decision-making
abilities. You may be assigned a task to study a briefing file of documents, sometimes against a tight time constraint. You may then have
to write a response to a task assigned to you. The in-tray exercise is
an example of this type of assignment and usually involves, for
example, details of a fictitious but comparable organizational structure, policy documents and reports on performance, e-mails from
imaginary colleagues, and letters from suppliers and customers.
You will be expected to read the background information and then

make recommendations to your line manager in response to a series of e-mail-style questions. Your time at the centre might involve the following in addition to one or more interviews.

Written assignments

These look at how well you can structure an argument and examine a number of options, recommending one. Make sure your keyboard skills are up to scratch. Don't overuse bullet points. Start with a summary and avoid quoting from the background information; rather, restate it in your own words. Offer clear, succinct statements of relevant data and reference sources. Take care with your grammar, spelling and punctuation.

Group exercises and presentations

Show that you can listen by making lots of eye contact and nodding in agreement. Take account of the contributions of others. Make as good a case as you can for the view that you are presenting. Don't start or get sucked into an argument, but if one occurs help make peace between the parties. Be enthusiastic even when discussing very mundane issues. Make absolutely sure you have sufficient evidence to back up what you plan to say and include plenty of figures. Keep your contributions to the point and spell out the relevance of anything you include that is not immediately significant to the discussion.

If you are invited to an assessment centre, the best approach is to set out to enjoy the day! They should do absolutely everything they can to make you feel at ease, and you can look forward to the chance to meet other candidates. Yes, it will be mentally challenging and tiring, but attend determined to give it your best shot and that way you will maximize your chances of coming out of the day with a job offer.

Written assessments, presentations, group exercises – all these test, among a number of things, your verbal reasoning skills, both written and spoken. You will most often face them at an assessment centre. You are invited to attend with a group of other applicants and will spend many hours in the company of representatives of the prospective employer and recruitment professionals, and you will be subjected to a range of assignments and interviews. It is not uncommon for the event to be held at a hotel and in some instances you may be invited to arrive the night before and be provided with overnight accommodation.

For obvious reason of cost, these events feature late in the recruitment process when the vast majority of candidates have been eliminated. If you are invited to one, congratulate yourself for getting through to this late stage. Many other applicants will have been disappointed. You can take it that the employer is very interested in you and is prepared to invest a considerable sum of money in taking a long, careful look at your potential. They will seek to use the event to form as objective an assessment of you as they can. In their eyes you will no longer be another application form or test paper result, but an individual they want to meet and get to know. They will also want you to be interested in them and to have thought carefully about why you want to join their organization. To answer this question properly you will need to have undertaken a careful look at the company, its services or products, and sector or sectors of operation. Unfortunately it is no longer sufficient to tell a prospective employer that you have had a look at its website. Attend armed with the benefits of a careful look at the organization overall, the section in which you would like to be placed and the position for which you have applied.

The time you spend and what you do at an assessment centre will vary from centre to centre and between recruitment campaigns. The experience may also vary slightly between candidates because some will, for example, undertake the interview first, followed by a written exercise, while others will undertake the written assignment first and then the interview. Things are organized in this way to manage resources efficiently and to reduce the time you spend hanging around waiting your turn. Organizations will inform you of an outline of what your day at the centre will comprise. You can glean a lot of very useful information from what you are sent, especially any information about the competencies examined. Read between the lines and you will be able to decide on the approach you will take.

An example of what such a day might include

The most important thing to take with you when you attend the centre is suitable ID. For reasons of test security, administrators will want to be able to confirm that no one is impersonating you and attending on your behalf. Read carefully and follow the instructions on your invitation and contact the organizers if you have any questions. They will provide you with everything you need or are allowed in terms of pens, scrap paper, calculators and so on. It would be a big mistake to arrive late for your appointment, so locate the centre and make sure you can find it with time to spare.

Many assessment events are organized with a number of common components. These include:

- *Group exercises.* These are sometimes called role-play exercises. In a group of usually five people you discuss a series of subjects. Before joining the group you are given a topic and briefing notes, and are allowed time to prepare. In the exercise you take turns introducing topics and have to discuss consensually. Assessors observe.

- *Presentations.* You're given a brief and time to prepare your topic. You then present this topic to an assessor, followed by questions. There are likely to be observers making notes.

- *Written exercises.* You're given a booklet of documents from different sources (press reports, semi-technical documents, etc) sometimes amounting to a lot of material. You read all the background information and assess it against a number of given criteria. You write up your findings, make recommendations and evaluate your decisions. The exercise is most likely to be completed on a PC.

- *Interviews.* The day is bound to include one or more panel interviews. You will face a panel of up to three people; one will lead. If you are applying for a professional or technical role you may face a technical interview as well.

These assessments will be competency-based. This means that the assignment will be used to test a given list of behaviour traits that are taken to be indicative of a desired quality. These might include any number of features such as communication skills, drive, decision making, relationship building, teamwork and so on.

The relationships between the various assignments and the competencies are likely to be set out on a matrix like the table shown here.

No.	Competency tested:	Determination	Development of ideas	Decision making	Planning	Team work	Written communication
1	Group exercise	*	*		*	*	*
2	Written exercise			*	*		*
3	Presentation		*	*			
4	Interview	*				*	

This table shows the link between an assessment and the competencies it is used to investigate. In practice, more competencies would be investigated than shown here. It is common for candidates to be told the competencies that will be investigated and, as already mentioned, this information can be used to plan your approach to the assessments.

Below I consider in more detail and offer insights and tips on how best to approach group exercises, presentations, written exercises and self-assessment exercises. A mock assessment centre can be found at www.gradjobs.co.uk.

The group exercise or role play

The topic or topics you are assigned to discuss vary from company to company, but you will find that group exercises are fundamentally similar in that you will be one of a number of candidates and you must engage in consensual discussion.

1. Preparation time

Group exercises start with time to prepare. During the preparation time, list points that you feel are very important and make sure that these come up in the discussion. Don't worry if someone raises one of your points before you got the chance to make it; just contribute to its discussion and help develop the issue. Sometimes you will get to meet the other candidates before the exercise starts; if you do, use this time to get to know them. You most likely will be told not to appoint a chairperson. Aim to play to your strengths. If maths is your thing, use the data they give you to work out some relevant figures (you should include figures even if maths is not your thing). It is vital to listen to others. They will be looking to see if your input helps to move the group forward, and whether you help the group to achieve its objectives.

In some cases you are given a great deal of briefing information – almost more than you can read in the time allowed. If this is the case, review the material quickly and keep your notes very brief. You might decide on an assessment tool to help in the handling of the briefing papers; examples include SWOT and PEST (Strengths, Weaknesses, Opportunities, Threats; and Political, Economic, Social, Technological). Another commonly used tool is the spider diagram, which is great for speed, recall and the emphasis of connections. Prepare these tools and think through these strategies before the day.

If you find that you do not have enough time to read all the background material, then decide what you want to say and use the time you have to make absolutely sure you have sufficient evidence to back up what you plan to say. Don't forget to include figures.

You are likely to be briefed as a group, and these are the people with whom you will discuss the topics. If it is appropriate and the opportunity presents itself, take the trouble to get to know some of the group. This will really help with any nervousness you may suffer. You will find it so much easier to have a constructive conversation with someone you have talked to before.

2. The discussion

The discussion will be observed and notes taken by the assessors; it may even be recorded on video. Push all this out of your mind as much as possible and keep your thoughts on the group, its objective and the discussion.

Try to avoid taking notes during the exercise. If you really must take notes, keep them extremely brief – just one-word notes – as you really do not want the invigilator to notice that you are 'looking down'. You want them to notice lots of eye contact and nods in agreement and to conclude that you can listen and have under-stood the significance of the contribution of others by modifying your position to take account of their contribution.

If you can, and the opportunity presents itself, speak first so that you make the first impression and demonstrate drive. Don't worry if your position is entirely different from everyone else's; you are being assessed on how you make your case, not what case you are making. So set out to make as good a case as you can for the view that you are representing, but also point out its weaknesses. Make sure you are enthusiastic even when discussing what might seem very mundane issues.

Be assertive in getting your points across, but be very careful not to stray into language that could be taken as aggressive. Listen as well as talk. Do make lots of eye contact and do nod in agreement, but don't shake your head or demonstrate your disagreement through body language. Consider making explicit reference to how you have modified your case to take into account the contributions of others. Do this by, for example, offering supportive summaries of others' contributions and then adding a further relevant point of your own.

Recognize the talents and merit in other people's contribution without diminishing your own. Use 'us' and 'we' to emphasize the collective purpose. Suggest criteria to clarify and evaluate the project. Help draw out quieter candidates by creating the space for them to speak. Do this by helping to ensure that everyone has a say. Show decisiveness and leadership qualities but avoid adopting the role of chair.

Don't take criticism personally. Don't start or get sucked into an argument, but in the unlikely event that one occurs, try to help make peace between the parties. This is important and a point on which many otherwise good candidates fail, so be sure to show empathy and go out of your way to resolve tension or disputes that arise between the other parties.

Be prepared to adopt the suggestions of others over your own, as this will be taken as an indication of your willingness to support another's project, of flexibility and of a talent in the building of relationships. Be constructive in your contributions and be supportive of others in your group. Keep your contributions to the point and spell out the relevance if you refer to something not immediately significant to the issue under discussion. Remember to back up all your points with facts and figures from the background material.

3. Self-assessment of your performance

It is common for you to be asked to complete a self-assessment of your performance at an assessment centre. Take this exercise seriously as it is often scored and counts towards your overall mark. If appropriate, comment on both what you learnt from it and on how you might improve, were you to attend the event or take the exercise again. Keep your self-criticism positive but be sure it is genuine. You might comment on, for example, how productive your relationship building was, the impact of your communication, or how the group could have better developed the assignment.

Many candidates find critical self-assessment a challenge; we are all so used to hiding our weaknesses and promoting our strengths. But realize that otherwise very strong candidates fail because they have not been open enough about their weaknesses and have not taken the opportunity to describe the strategies they have devised to address them.

Presentations

There is a lot you can do before the day to prepare for your presentation.

1. Plan something to say on core issues relevant to most subjects

Every sector of industry has issues that are relevant to pretty much every scenario. They depend on the industry of course, but might include recent legislation, the environment, health and safety, equality of opportunity, inclusiveness of people with disabilities (don't only think wheelchairs but include all types of disability) and social inclusion generally. There are bound to be cross-cutting themes relevant to the organization to which you have applied, so research them. The opportunity may arise where you can refer to these issues and gain valuable points.

2. Decide in advance how you might structure your presentation

You are unlikely to know the subject of your presentation until a short time before you have to make it, but this does not mean that you cannot do some preparation on the possible structure you intend to use. In the introduction you may want to summarize what you intend to go on to say and then in your conclusion review what you have said. There are some very good publications on the making of successful presentations; they may be worth a look.

You might decide to start by stating succinctly the assignment and go on to describe why addressing the issue is useful or necessary. If appropriate you could then review the file material (people, budget, rules) or background. Headings after that point might include Actions, Recommendations, Alternatives, Conclusion. Do not forget that it is essential that you show enthusiasm throughout.

3. Practise getting your timing right

You may not yet know how long you will have to present, but all the same it is worth practising how much you can say effectively in the usual time slots allocated in these exercises. On the day you will be allocated something between 10 and 20 minutes and you do not want to finish short or overrun. To get it right you need to have some experience of how long it will take to present a series of points with impact. Try to say too much or too little and you may end up disappointed with your presentation. Listen to a few public speakers on the radio, for example, and study how they make a point with impact and how long it takes them. You do not want to find yourself unable to cover all the points you planned to make and to be told to stop before you have made your concluding remarks.

4. The briefing and preparation time

You are often given a number of subjects from which to choose and are always provided with a briefing pack on the subject and told the time you have to prepare your presentation. Don't make the mistake of thinking you have to comment on all the subjects, including the ones you did not select. So, at the briefing, get absolutely clear in your mind the nature of the assignment and if in doubt ask someone for clarification. Be warned that it is common for the amount of time allowed for studying the background papers to be very tight. These events are sometimes organized so that the time allowed for reading the papers and preparing your presentation are combined, so be very careful not to spend too much time reading the papers and finding yourself with insufficient time to prepare your presentation.

Be sure to present the difficulties as well as the advantages of your approach to the topic. Often you are asked to provide something original on the subject. Even if you are not specifically asked to do this, it may be worth offering a novel aspect to your presentation, and then go on to examine the benefits and challenges to this aspect (don't forget to identify it as an original contribution). The relevance of everything you say should be clear or be explained. In practice, the invigilators don't so much care what you decide on but judge you on how you explain, justify and criticize it.

Once you have decided what to say, settle on your structure and make clear legible notes to which you can refer when making the presentation, and resolve to keep to it. Allocate an amount of time to each part of your presentation. Do not try to write out verbatim what you hope to cover. Even if you could manage it in the time allowed, the exercise is not one of you having to read your essay out loud. Instead, try numbering your points and commit these numbers and keywords belonging to the points to memory. Try labelling them with one-word reminders and memorizing these. Try anything that works for you and will help you recall the points you want to make without excessive reference to your notes.

Remember to work quickly, as you may find you have very little time to prepare for your presentation.

5. Your presentation

Nerves aside, your presentation is likely to be as good or bad as your preparation, both before the day and during the preparation time. They are not expecting a polished public performance, but do be sure to speak clearly, make eye contact and try to keep reference to your notes to a minimum. Do think on your feet and adapt what you say as you speak, then revert back to your structure. Keep an eye on the time and try as much as possible to keep to the limits you set to speaking on each part of your presentation. If you find yourself going over time, drop some points. As already said, it is more important to deliver a timely presentation than be asked to stop before you have reached your conclusions. You are very likely to get the opportunity to raise further points and add details in the question and answer session that follows.

6. Follow-up questions/discussion

In these exercises it is common for more time to be spent answering questions and discussing what you said with the invigilator than you spent making your presentation.

It will help if you think of this time more as a brainstorming session than a cross-examination. So approach it with an open, curious mind rather than risk being perceived as defensive. During questions, the invigilator may follow up your response and keep asking follow-up questions until they feel they have the measure of you. At some point they will have decided whether you have made the grade, but they may still keep asking questions until you run out of things to say. Don't let this undermine your self-confidence and don't take offence. When the next line of questioning begins, it's a fresh start; a new line of enquiry, and you should have a different line of responses. Avoid falling back to a previous response, ie avoid repeating yourself. At all times make sure your response is relevant to the question and the line of enquiry. Listening skills are as important here as they are in the group exercise. Expect there to be one person who leads the questions and one or more others who mainly observe and take notes.

7. Self-assessment

If you are required to complete a self-assessment of your performance in the presentation exercise then take it seriously and complete it to the best of your ability; a score of what you write may feature as a part of your overall assessment. See the note on self-assessment, above.

Written exercises

1. Overview

These are tests of your ability to handle information, organize it and communicate in writing. You will be presented with a file of papers that provide information on a subject. It may include conflicting information that you have to evaluate and make recommendations about. Your task is to analyse the papers and prepare a note that builds a balanced and convincing case. To do this you will need to compare and contrast the options, using the stated criteria or proposing your own, and explain convincingly the reasons for your recommendation. These exercises are nearly always completed on a computer, so make sure your keyboard skills are up to scratch.

2. Planning in advance

Again, you can undertake some useful preparation before the day. One thing to consider is the style of approach that you adopt. This decision will depend in part on your background and your strengths; it is obvious that you should play to these. It should also be dependent on the role for which you are applying. By this I mean, if you are applying for a role in business then adopt a business style of report writing, with an executive summary stating the recommendation and summarizing the whole document, the main body and then the conclusion. If you are applying to an academic institution then a university style of report may be more appropriate and, if you can, adopt an elegant, fluid, readable written style. Research on the internet the style of reports and publications used in the organization or industrial sector in which they operate and, if you are confident to do so, adopt this style in the written exercise. That way you will appear well suited to the position. If producing a written document is really not your thing, consider using (but not excessively) bullet points and underlined headings to help convey your message. Illustrate points, where applicable: they will be far more convincing. If you find that you have not included numbers in your note, then you have probably not done as well as you could, so where practical back up and provide numerical evidence for what you say. Many organizations are looking for you to provide evidence of the case or point you make, so refer to figures or passages in the background paper and remember to source references.

Before the day it may be useful to give thought to analytical tools or processes to which you might refer or use in the exercise. Some have already been mentioned, including SWOT and PEST (see page 26). Consider if there are any core issues to which you might make reference in your paper that are applicable to most issues in the industrial sector to which you are applying. Look at reports and studies on the internet to identify possible issues. They might include, for example, equality of opportunity, reaching the hard to reach or challenging members of our society, or the contributions and/or threats technological advances might bring.

A common question asked is, how much should I write? The answer is that, within reason, what matters is not how much you write but what you write. Some assignments stipulate the extent expected, others do not. When no extent is indicated, set out to write enough to get the job done well. Don't write without good purpose, and take care to use the correct grammar, spelling and punctuation. Write too much and you increase the risk of errors and have less time to find any errors you may have made.

3. The briefing and preparation time

When you come to take the assignment it is very likely that you will be briefed on the exercise and provided with background or briefing paper. You may have a lot of information to go through and the time allowed to complete this part of the task may be tight. Be sure not to get caught out by the time limit. Get clear the aim of the exercise as explained to you and, first and foremost, use the time allowed to obtain the information necessary to serve the objective of the assignment. Then set about deciding the line to take in your paper and the structure that you will adopt.

4. The written assignment itself

Much of what you have done during your education and working career to date will serve you well in a written exercise. Take confidence from the fact that you have the skills to succeed in this assessment and apply what you have prepared before the day and during the briefing and preparation time. Although the written assignment is almost certainly to be administered on a PC, think back to the written exams at school or university for an idea of what to expect and insight into the best approach. Start with a note of the structure that you have decided to adopt and then use your time to implement that plan. Take care over grammar and spelling. Remember the invigilators are looking to see how well you can structure an argument and examine a number of options, recommending one. Where appropriate, use illustrations to make your points; back up what you say with figures; consider rather than quote from the background information, paraphrasing it or restating the passage in your own words. Demonstrate your ability at handling numerical information by offering clear, succinct restatements of relevant data in the background information. Remember to reference sources. Be convincing while remaining impartial and objective.

Chapter 2
The winning approach

When used for selection purposes, psychometric tests of verbal skills are a type of competition in which you must score better than other candidates. If passing is important, you must make a major commitment in terms of the time you devote to practising in the weeks leading up to the test. Other candidates are bound to be doing this, so if you don't you risk failure. You must also adopt a winning mindset.

Your approach to these tests is critical to success. You have considerable influence over your score; in fact the outcome is largely dependent on how you conduct yourself on the day and the degree to which you arrive fully prepared.

See the test as an opportunity to demonstrate your true potential. This is the winning mindset. Avoid feelings of resentment or a fear of failure whereby you commit less than your full worth. If passing the test means that you can realize a life goal then you have every reason to try your best and show the employer just how good you really are. Preparation is the key.

The best-scoring candidate arrives very well prepared. You should too. Attend fully aware of the demands of the test. The computer program or test administrator will introduce a number of familiarization questions before the start of the actual test. These should be entirely familiar. The top scoring candidates are the ones looking forward to the test: they have confidence in themselves and the key to confidence is practice. They realize that they have nothing to lose if they give it their best and go for it.

Practice before the test is essential and makes a significant difference to your likely score. Practice means that you are likely to make fewer mistakes and are faster against often tight time constraints. Importantly, practice allows you to revise forgotten rules and develop a good exam technique. This involves becoming familiar with the format of the questions and maximizing your score through educated guessing. Everyone's score will improve through practice.

First, become entirely familiar with each aspect of the test. The employer or test publisher should send you or refer you to a description of it, the type of questions, the number of them, and the time allowed. Next find sufficient practice material. This book is a very good start and for many candidates will prove sufficient. Only spend time practising questions that are a lot like the real questions in terms of the level of difficulty and competencies examined.

If you face a very competitive situation in which many hundreds apply, it's inevitable that a great many very able candidates will be failed. To avoid this fate be prepared to undertake a significant amount of practice. Even then it may take a number of attempts before you pass. I know some accomplished people who have never failed anything in their life before they are invited to sit an advanced psychometric test in one of the big competitions. Failure can come as quite a surprise and may require them to up their game a little. The answer is practice and, if need be, a lot of it.

Be sure to concentrate on your personal challenges. We all like to spend time on things at which we excel, but when it comes to a test it pays to focus on improving your areas of weakness first and foremost. If the rules of English usage have always been a bit of an enigma, if you struggle to appreciate the fine distinctions drawn in tests of comprehension, then give yourself sufficient time and set about mastering what you have previously managed without. Keep going over explanations and examples until you understand the principles fully, then keep practising at realistic questions in exam-like conditions. It may prove boring, painful even, but it will work. Your score will quite quickly improve.

Develop – or rediscover – a good exam technique. This demands a balance between speed and accuracy. Some very good candidates will need to unlearn a thoughtful, considered approach to issues. You can actually think too deeply or take too few risks in these tests. Practise realistic questions under the pressure of time. When appropriate, look to suggested answers for clues and practise informed guessing, where you eliminate some of the suggested answers and then guess from those that remain. If you face a test administered on a computer or online, be sure your keyboard skills are up to scratch.

If it is some years since you last sat a test, practise at keeping a check on how long you spend on any one question and keep going right up to the very last second. You have to get the balance right between speed and accuracy. This takes practice, especially as you are likely to face some anxiety during the real test and therefore be prone to making mistakes. Accept the fact that you will get some questions wrong: it is better that you attempt every question and risk getting some wrong than check every answer twice only to be told that you have run out of time. If you reach a series of difficult questions, don't lose heart but keep going. The next section may comprise something at which you excel, so never give up. Practise managing your time so that you attempt every question, and apply educated guesses to any you cannot answer.

Devise a study plan well in advance of the test date and include the following steps.

Step 1

Make sure that you know exactly what to expect at each stage of the test and if it is on screen, ensure you are familiar with the screen icons and format so that you are able to concentrate on the questions.

Step 2

Make an honest assessment of your strengths and weaknesses. To prepare thoroughly for any test you should first concentrate your efforts on improving the areas in which you are weakest. As objectively as possible assess the extent to which your area(s) of personal challenge will let you down. You can use the practice tests in this book for this. That way you can observe your progress and focus on the parts of the assessment in which you did least well. Repeat this process of assessment regularly during your revision.

Step 3

Plan a programme of practice. Decide how much time you will spend preparing for the challenge. The sooner you start the better, and a little but often is better than occasional long sessions of practice. Some candidates may only need to spend a number of weeks revising what they have previously mastered; others will need to undertake a far more extensive programme of revision.

The assessment described in step 2 will tell you how much of a challenge the test represents. Be sure to take the challenge seriously and avoid the trap of promising yourself that you will start tomorrow. For some candidates, tomorrow never comes or comes far too late.

For many candidates facing an advance battery of tests, a winning plan is likely to involve work over a minimum of two months, twice and preferably three times a week. If English is not your first language, or if to date you have accomplished much despite never mastering the rules of English usage, then be prepared to set aside more time than this and over a longer period.

Step 4

Obtain every piece of practice material available. Many candidates facing psychometric tests cannot find sufficient relevant material on which to practise. This book has been written especially for tests at the advanced level and you should make the most of it.

As I have said, some candidates will need more material than found here, and good sources include the following:

For material that introduces and leads up to the level found in graduate and management tests, try these books in the Kogan Page testing series: *The Ultimate Psychometric Test Book,* 2006, and *How to Pass Graduate Psychometric Tests,* third edition, 2007.

For more material at advanced level I recommend *The Official Guide for GMAT review*, Graduate Admissions Council (GMAT is the test used to select for places on MBA courses in many business schools). From the Kogan Page testing series, try: *How To Pass the GMAT,* 2007, and *The Graduate Psychometric Test Workbook*, 2nd edition, 2010.

Step 5

Undertake two sorts of practice. First, to get the most from your practice, begin working in a relaxed situation, without constraints of time, reviewing examples of questions, and working out the answers so as to become familiar with the demands of typical questions. Feel free to review answers and explanations and refer to textbooks, dictionaries and a thesaurus as you wish. You will find lots of this sort of warm-up practice in the first five chapters.

Then, once you have reviewed the challenge you should start to practise under realistic test conditions. This involves putting aside the dictionary and thesaurus and working against the clock without help or interruption. The purpose is to develop a good exam technique and to improve your stamina and endurance. Learn not to spend too long on any one question, and practise educated guessing. You will find realistic practice tests in Chapters 6 and 7, along with interpretations of your score. Answers and explanation to all the questions in this book can be found in Chapter 8.

To get the most out of this second sort of practice, set yourself the personal challenge of trying to beat your last score each time you take a test. You will need to try very hard and take the challenge seriously if you are to really succeed in beating your previous best score every time. When you finish a test you should feel mentally tired but satisfied that you are creating a realistic test 'feel'.

Use this book even if it does not contain practice questions of the sort found in the real tests you face. Even if the style of questions is different, the competencies you are practising are the same. So use the material in this book and you will still improve your score in the real verbal reasoning test.

Chapter 3
110 Warm-up questions

Tests of verbal ability

These tests are by far the most common and this book comprises hundreds of practice questions. You can find free online examples at www.mikebryon.com, www.shl.com and www.psl.co.uk (note that you have to register at the last two sites to receive the free practice questions). As previously mentioned, these involve multiple-choice tests of your work-related verbal abilities organized as tests of your command of English usage, reading comprehension, written assignments, group discussions or presentations. If the test is multiple-choice, the verbal reasoning test is likely to comprise only one or two of a battery of sub-tests set one after the other against a tight time constraint. The battery is very likely to include tests of other abilities in addition to your verbal reasoning, so be sure to include practice for all of them in your preparation time.

This chapter contains 110 warm-up questions. They are organized as five practice types that investigate your vocabulary, comprehension or knowledge of English usage. This style of question is less common than it used to be, but still prevalent. If you are applying for a range of graduate or management jobs then at some stage you are bound to face a test similar to this. Practice will make a big difference to your performance in that test. If you face a highly competitive advanced test in which you must score well against many other candidates, then this practice is essential. Some candidates need only revise what they have not practised for a few years; others will have to set aside a quite significant amount of time and work on this and the further practice material recommended below.

These are warm-up questions in that they are not all at the advanced level. This is intentional and allows the questions to help the greatest number of readers. You should expect to get the vast majority of these questions right. If you find that you cannot achieve this level of accuracy, be prepared to undertake a quite significant amount of practice to ensure that you reach the standard demanded by advanced verbal reasoning tests.

Even if you do not face a test of this type, use this material to develop a good exam technique. If you prefer, take these exercises under exam-type conditions. Time limits have been suggested for the sets of questions.

Hundreds more practice questions at the advanced level are available from the Kogan Page testing series, in particular: *How to Pass Graduate Psychometric Tests,* third edition, 2007, *The Graduate Psychometric Test Workbook*, second edition, 2010, and *How to Pass the GMAT*, 2007.

Word link: opposites

With this style of question your task is to find the word in the list that is the opposite of the first word. The question setter will deliberately try to mislead you, so take care not to fall for the premeditated traps. One common trap is to offer a word in the list that means the same as the question word rather than the opposite, in the expectation that you will forget the task and identify the synonym rather than the antonym as the answer. Use the following 10 examples to become completely familiar with this task.

Doing well in these questions is all about possessing a wide vocabulary and having the confidence to use it. If you find them very easy, that is fantastic but don't make the mistake of not practising. In a test of this type there will be far more questions than the time allows you to answer. The high-scoring candidate will be the one who can get the right answer without double-checking or taking too much time reflecting on the suggested answers. So do not make the mistake of thinking you will achieve a high score in the real test just because you can do well in these questions without any time pressure.

If you prefer to attempt these questions against the clock, allow 4 minutes for the 10 questions.

1   faithful

inaccurate
faithless
authentic
fake

Answer [   ]

2   lift

boast
impose
plagiarize
elevate

Answer [   ]

3   opaque

transparent
obscure
perplexing
unintelligible

Answer [   ]

4   hypothesize

posit
propose
refute
conjecture

Answer [   ]

5 restrain
enable
prevent
control
enact

Answer

6 emphatic
denial
vehement
conclusive
narrow

Answer

7 laconic
verbose
terse
uncommunicative
reticent

Answer

8 straightforward
forthcoming
multifaceted
forthwith
ahead

Answer

9 opulent
poverty
sumptuous
spartan
copious

Answer

10 nominal
rent
ostensible
symbolic
real

Answer

Word link: synonyms

In this style of question your task is to find two words, one from each list, closest in meaning or with the strongest connection. As with the last style of question, this is a test of your vocabulary and your confidence in it. Reading widely and practising are the key to doing well in tests of this sort. If you wish to experience these questions under test-like conditions, allow yourself 4 minutes to complete the 10 questions. If you get any of the questions wrong, be sure to look up the word in a dictionary.

11   A. wholly   D. unconditionally
       B. partially   E. in the interim
       C. momentarily   F. temporarily

                              Answer _____

12   A. statute   D. static
       B. consistent   E. inactive
       C. stable   F. statutory

                              Answer _____

13   A. hopeless   D. solvent
       B. confident   E. doubtful
       C. secure   F. buoyant

                              Answer _____

14   A. outcry   D. rejection
       B. overt   E. brazen
       C. hyped   F. acceptance

                              Answer _____

15   A. perplex   D. clarify
       B. faceted   E. complex
       C. elucidate   F. simple

                              Answer _____

16 A. rough
    B. smooth
    C. forceful
    D. weak
    E. broad
    F. truthful

Answer [   ]

17 A. annual
    B. annul
    C. biannual
    D. rescind
    E. requital
    F. habitual

Answer [   ]

18 A. scarcely
    B. narrowly
    C. notoriously
    D. erroneously
    E. decently
    F. hardly

Answer [   ]

19 A. footsie
    B. standalone
    C. footloose
    D. roaming
    E. footer
    F. connected

Answer [   ]

20 A. belittle
    B. empathetic
    C. emphatic
    D. emphasize
    E. invigorate
    F. commiserative

Answer [   ]

Find the new word

In this type of test your task is to find a four-letter word *or words* that are made up by combining the last few letters of one of the given words with the first few letters of the next word. Most of the answers are everyday terms with which you are entirely familiar, although towards the end of the exercise some more obscure words are introduced. No archaic or informal words, abbreviations or regional spellings are used, and as a general rule if the word is not one of the exceptions mentioned and it is found in the *Concise Oxford English Dictionary*, then it is considered correct. There are 30 questions of this type – you should be able to complete them in 10 minutes.

21   graduate   asylum   veterinary

Answer

22   express   often   exposure

Answer

23   tycoon   lyrical   manifest

Answer

24   carriage   oscillate   archaeology

Answer

25   kangaroo   muscle   senior

Answer

26   induction   Celsius   errant

Answer

27   seminar   ear bashing   dysphasia

Answer

28   immense   immunize   rocket

Answer

29   facilitate   straight   extenuate

Answer

30   economist   ownership   packet

Answer

31 pasta   petulant   gladden

Answer [   ]

32 window   heyday   earache

Answer [   ]

33 alcove   intravenous   hopeful

Answer [   ]

34 Cadillac   elliptic   onward

Answer [   ]

35 alibi   ascertain   chaffinch

Answer [   ]

36 chose   choose   cuttlefish

Answer [   ]

37 pump   awning   insensible

Answer [   ]

38 multitude   edifice   educational

Answer [   ]

39 marshal   cub   aitchbone

Answer [   ]

40 persona   crestfallen   honour

Answer [   ]

41 immanent   Kawasaki   mammal

Answer [   ]

42 broccoli   fearful   hackney

Answer [   ]

43   essential   flour   oleander

Answer [   ]

44   kerbstone   apocalypse   education

Answer [   ]

45   demonstrable   Adriatic   kaleidoscope

Answer [   ]

46   token   factive   toilet

Answer [   ]

47   abnormal   lychee   preparatory

Answer [   ]

48   digamma   tearaway   incriminate

Answer [   ]

49   thali   ferment   microscope

Answer [   ]

50   bourgeois   embody   notability

Answer [   ]

Word swap

In these questions, two words have been interchanged so that the first word has been moved to the place in the sentence of the second, and the second moved to the location in the sentence of the first word. No other change to the sentence has occurred. It is your task to identify the two words that have been swapped. You should record your answer by writing the two words in the answer box. Be sure to record the words in the order that they occur in the question (that is, the incorrect order). Allow yourself 10 minutes in which to complete these questions.

51 The only equipment really needed in the kitchen is a couple of sharp pans and some stainless steel knives.

Answer [   ]

52 If the rooftops of each house in the United States were covered in photo-catalytic cells then every household would have at its disposal the hydrogen equivalent of over 10 litres of gasoline a day.

Answer [   ]

53 Only if your guest is on the name list will you be allowed in prior to the start of the show.

Answer [   ]

54 You must pass the actual test before you can take the written driving test.

Answer [   ]

55 It is quite untrue fact pigs are dirty, they are in that very clean animals.

Answer [   ]

56 The very strong traffic in winter often means the bridge has to be closed to winds.

Answer [   ]

57 Some spiders have an irrational fear of people, even very small ones.

Answer [   ]

58 One of the most important problems of an MP's job is meeting constituents and discussing their aspects.

Answer [   ]

59 Two parties who want to benefit with one another both communicate from coming to a common agreement about the words they use.

Answer [   ]

60 Keeping abreast of essential affairs is current for any modern writer.

Answer [   ]

61 At a rung hour of the evening a bell was fixed, signalling that all fires were to be extinguished.

Answer [   ]

62 When you take a careful look at how a major city hasn't changed over 100 years you are immediately struck not by the way it has changed but by the ways it has, in particular, the broad patterns of socio-economic class remain the same as do many local socio-economic characteristics.

Answer [   ]

63 If you are one of the many people these days with more complex affairs, for example, someone with professional children from more than one marriage, then a will is essential and probably requires the services of a dependent if it is to be drawn up in a way that ensures that it survives your death unchallenged.

Answer [   ]

64 Countries are slowly realizing that there is no such thing as no immigration and zero such thing as a non-porous border.

Answer [   ]

65 Worldwide only a few thousand people are estimated to live a truly subsistence life, most have been forced to abandon their traditional lifestyle practised for millennia and have had to settle down in villages to live a life of hunting combined with nomadic farming.

Answer

66 Widespread help from parents and family members which always cast doubt on the value of examinations in has home-completed assignments contribute to the grade awarded.

Answer

67 Biologists have long known of the standard of single-celled plants that can break water molecules apart and release hydrogen and oxygen gas; the hope is that a microorganism can be found capable of generating hydrogen gas in sufficient quantities to reach the existence of 10 per cent water-splitting efficiency.

Answer

68 It is a fact that good news is always much more newsworthy than bad news and so we hear a constant stream of numerical 'facts' purporting to show that life is indeed grim.

Answer

69 For the vast majority of dealers and their customers the celebrated super colourful stamps are the subject only of catalogues and magazine articles; their domain is more likely to be the newly issued expensive commemorative stamps printed in the millions by national post offices.

Answer

70 A problem that was notorious 100 years ago as somewhere frequented by drunks and members of the criminal class may well be found to suffer the same challenges, only the language used to describe the place will have changed and perhaps the problem will be attributed today to drugs rather than alcohol, and alienated youth rather than a criminal class.

Answer

71 People no longer passively share media content and are beginning to value their own opinion and offer it alongside that of the supposed experts and authorities when they post online rates, consume podcasts and contribute to threads on collaborative sites.

Answer

72 The secret involved in a paper plane are as complex as the principles behind any plane, but the aerodynamics to one built in paper is ease of construction, folds that give strength, a correctly located centre of balance, minimum drag and maximum lift.

Answer

73 Hong Kong is one of the international cities with a leading world's financial centre and a gateway for trade and investment between China and the rest of the world.

Answer

74 A laser emits an electric bulb which emits light in all directions and over a broad spectrum unlike light from a narrow part of the wavelength and in a well-defined beam.

Answer

75 The day will have a cloudy start with some light rain but will become brighter and drier by afternoon and there will be some sunny spells in the midday.

Answer

76 Ever enthusiastic Christopher Columbus brought tobacco back to Spain from the Americas, Spaniards have been among the world's most since.

Answer

77 Faced with the spiralling cost of medical care and double-digit increases in premiums for the fifth year running, US insurers are desperately looking for astronomical ways to tackle the innovative cost of medical insurance.

Answer [   ]

78   The landscape for the contorted, dreamlike inspiration painted by Salvador Dali was the small fishing village of Cadagues on the Costa Brava in Spain.

Answer [   ]

79   The word laser is the amplification for light acronym by stimulated emission of radiation.

Answer [   ]

80   Jack Digby married an actress and became a father and actor himself and played the model in the film 'Four Weddings and a Funeral'.

Answer [   ]

Sentence sequence

You may well be familiar with numerical sequence questions where you have to calculate the next number in a series or complete a series. This type of question is the verbal equivalent. Each question comprises four sentences, **A** to **D**, but the order in which they were originally written has been lost and the sentences are now in the wrong order. Your task is to put the sentences into the correct order or original order. Attempt to do these questions in 15 minutes.

81   A. The walking season never ends; indeed each month brings its own character and invites you to repeat a walk at different times of the year.

   B. It is ideal for families, who do not need to join a club in order to do it.

C. Walking and close contact with the real, living world are essential parts of growing up, especially in the television age.

D. Walking is a natural activity that requires little in the way of money and gives enjoyment without a competitive element.

Answer

82 A. It may have as many as 40 or 50 buckets, each capable of raising 1 cubic metre of spoil.

B. A dredger of this kind will easily raise 40,000 cubic metres of spoil in a week.

C. A bucket dredger is a particularly useful machine because it can dredge quite accurately to a required depth and leaves the ground over which it has worked fairly level.

D. If the cutting edges of the buckets are fitted with teeth the dredger can even cut and raise soft rock.

Answer

83 A. Arsine, a colourless, poisonous gas compound of arsenic and hydrogen, is used as a doping agent for semiconductors and as a military poison gas.

B. The compounds of arsenic are mostly poisonous.

C. Among the most important commercially are arsenious oxide (white arsenic), used in pesticides and in the manufacture of glass and the preserving of animal hides; and arsenic pentoxide, which is a major ingredient in the production of insecticides, herbicides and weedkillers, and metal adhesives.

D. Arsenic acid, lead arsenate, and calcium arsenate are all important in agriculture in sterilizing soils and controlling pests.

Answer

84   A. When the wax is removed, only the areas that were not waxed are coloured.

   B. The cloth is then dyed and dried.

   C. Instead of painting or printing a colour directly on a cloth, as in most patterned fabrics, the worker covers parts of the fabric with wax.

   D. The process used for batik is called resist dyeing.

Answer [   ]

85   A. Friction comes from the Latin word meaning 'rub'.

   B. Friction always occurs when two articles are moved so as to rub or chafe against one another.

   C. This resistance, or force which opposes motion, is called friction.

   D. When a heavy wooden box is pushed along the floor, resistance is set up between the box and the floor.

Answer [   ]

86   A. The eel-like hagfish has a very unpleasant way of life.

   B. Over 100 hagfish have been found in one large, dead fish.

   C. If the 'host' fish were alive originally, it slowly dies as its body is eaten away.

   D. It bores its way into the bodies of other fish – alive, dead or dying – and burrows through their flesh, eating as it goes.

Answer [   ]

87   A. The laws were written in the Sumerian language, in wedge-shaped letters called cruciform.

   B. Hammurabi, a wise and able ruler, was concerned with bringing order and justice to his kingdom.

   C. This was a collection of more than 280 laws, which he had inscribed on a great stone pillar.

D. He set up a strong central government and gathered all the laws of his kingdom into a great code.

Answer [   ]

88   A. (Australia, though larger, is not usually counted as an island.)

B. More than four-fifths of its area consists of a vast ice cap rising very gradually to a central dome, and only in the coastal regions can people live or plants grow.

C. Greenland is about 2,670 km from north to south, and over 1,050 km at its widest point east to west.

D. Greenland is the world's largest island and is located in the north Atlantic ocean, off the east coast of Canada.

Answer [   ]

89   A. A standard medicine such as paracetamol (acetaminophen) may help to lower or relieve aches and pains, though it won't alter the course of the illness.

B. Whooping cough and some of the other infections are caused by bacteria, in which case drugs may often help to fight the illness.

C. Chickenpox, measles, German measles and mumps are all caused by viruses.

D. Few drugs are effective against viruses, so the best treatment is to let the patient rest, as his or her body attacks and kills the viruses naturally.

Answer [   ]

90   A. With it, it is possible to build dams, foundations, tall slender bridges, high-rise buildings, and paved areas such as roads and airfield runways.

B. Cement is used in one of several ways in nearly every building in the Western world, and hundreds of millions of tonnes of cement are used throughout the world every year.

    C. Cement is one of the most versatile binders known to man.

    D. It is also used in the manufacture of building blocks, roofing tiles, and even things as thin as roofing sheet.

Answer

91 A. This is doubtful.

    B. Paintings made in the first half of the 18th century show the members of one clan in different tartans, and even one clansman with separate tartans for his coat, waistcoat and kilt, and it is unlikely that the clans kept strictly to particular tartans until the 19th century.

    C. The oldest known painting showing Highland dress dates from about 1660, and few earlier records are reliable.

    D. It is sometimes claimed that the different Scottish tartans served in ancient times to distinguish not only the different clans but also the ranks of the clansmen.

Answer

92 A. The body of the common African civet is about 90 cm long, a little less than the length of its bushy tail.

    B. The coarse grey fur is tinged with yellow and marked with black spots and bands.

    C. As a rule the civet lives in a hole in the ground, coming out mostly at night to search for rodents, birds and insects; it will also eat fruit.

    D. The civets of India and other parts of Asia, of which there are several kinds, are usually smaller and their fur is striped rather than spotted.

Answer

93 A. Nowadays, many people camp without 'roughing it', using caravans, campers or tents with all the modern comforts of home: a cooker, shower, toilet and even a television.

B. Tents have been used by people for thousands of years.

C. Explorers and mountain climbers have camped in some of the most remote and unfriendly places on earth.

D. They are still the chief homes for some, such as the wandering Bedouin of North Africa and Arabia.

Answer [   ]

94   A. Slow-speed film (50 ASA or less) reacts slowly to light and is used in very bright conditions, such as sun or snow.

B. Film comes in different 'speeds', given on the packet in ASA/ISO or DIN numbers.

C. The light passing through the lens of a camera acts on the light-sensitive chemicals in the film which, after being developed (or processed), produces a negative from which prints can be made.

D. Medium-speed film (50 to 125 ASA) is for normal sunny conditions, and fast-speed film (200 to 400 ASA) is best for cloudy or dim conditions.

Answer [   ]

95   A. The state has been made habitable by water, natural gas and hydroelectric power, mostly brought in from the outside, and by the invention of air conditioning.

B. Most of its landscape consists of rugged mountains, arid desert, mesas and buttes.

C. More than 300 ranges of mountains cross the state north to south.

D. Nevada is the driest state in the United States and one of the hottest.

Answer [   ]

96   A. At intervals along the mycelium, fruiting bodies, or sporophores, develop.

B. Mushrooms spread by spores that develop on the gills.

C. These grow into a massive network of underground threads (mycelium).

D. When the spores ripen they are released, and if they land in a warm, moist place they grow into thread-like chains of cells (hyphae).

Answer ☐

97 A. Some people are born with greater possibilities or 'potential intelligence' than others.

B. Intelligence is improved by learning.

C. It is no longer thought that intelligence is a general quality, underlying all behaviour and inherited wholly from our parents.

D. However, this potential may not develop unless it is encouraged and stimulated by influences surrounding the child from birth.

Answer ☐

98 A. This usually amounts to about £16,000.

B. Even so, some former MPs struggle to make ends meet.

C. On top of this, they receive a 'winding-up' allowance to take care of any unpaid staff, and research or other expenses.

D. MPs get golden handshakes and they are fairly generous, with payments of between 50 and 100 per cent of their annual £55,118 salary given to them when the electorate turns nasty.

Answer ☐

99 A. These include, for example, the use of diamonds in a dentist's drill.

B. The remainder are used for industrial purposes, that is for useful as distinct from decorative purposes.

C. Other applications of industrial diamonds are found in engineering, where tools with very hard surfaces are needed for cutting and grinding other hard surfaces.

D. Less than 50 per cent of rough diamonds are suitable for cutting and turning into jewellery.

Answer [   ]

100 A. Slowly, differences in ways of speaking become more and more marked, and these differences will eventually make a new dialect.

B. Dialects come about when people who have been living together and speaking to one another in the same way move apart.

C. Language changes, even as it is passed on from parents to children.

D. Separation of groups of people by a move across a physical barrier, such as a mountain or a river, can lead to different ways of speaking the same language.

Answer [   ]

101 A. The amount of work performed to bring about an energy change is exactly equal to the quantity of energy being converted into new forms.

B. The total energy at the end of any change is the same as the total energy before the change.

C. This is an important principle known as the conservation of energy.

D. Energy may be changed from one form to another, and work is the process that brings about the change.

Answer [   ]

102 A. Many of them reproduce so slowly that they are unable to make up for the numbers that are wiped out.

B. It is thought that one species becomes extinct every day, while many more become threatened.

C. Biologists estimate that 1 in 10 of all species is in danger of dying out.

D. That means there are at least a million endangered species of plants and animals.

Answer [   ]

103 A. Sometimes they are based on time – the worker being paid at a rate of so much an hour or so much a week; and sometimes they are based on articles produced – a shirt maker, for example, being paid at a rate of so much for every shirt made (piece work).

B. Payments of this type are usually controlled by law, so that the worker is protected against a bad employer who might try to pay all or nearly all the wages in kind.

C. Wages, or salaries, are payments by employers to their employees in return for work.

D. Wages are paid in money, but sometimes they include payments in kind, as when a caretaker is provided with a rent-free house and miners are given free or very cheap coal.

Answer [   ]

104 A. Throughout the world, techniques to measure pupil development and achievement have improved in recent years.

B. Standardized tests are used to a great extent.

C. These serve not only to compare a student with his or her fellow classmates but also to compare him or her with other students in the country at large.

D. The emphasis on individual differences and pupil interests has led to better methods of assessment.

Answer [   ]

105 A. This is known as the circular flow of income.

B. In economic life people are dependent on each other.

C. Whenever somebody spends, somebody else earns.

D. Macroeconomics is the study of how the whole of a country's economy works.

Answer [   ]

106 A. In fact the word 'echinoderm' means 'spiny-skinned'.

B. In sea urchins this is very obvious.

C. In many echinoderms these plates have knobs or spines on them that stick through the skin and give the creature a prickly appearance.

D. The skeleton is made of hard, chalky plates just under the skin.

Answer [   ]

107 A. The oceanic crust is only 6–8 km thick.

B. There are two kinds of crust.

C. The continental crust averages 35 km, but reaches a thickness of 60–70 km under high mountain ranges.

D. One kind, the oceanic crust, is beneath the oceans and seas, while the other, the continental crust, composes the continents.

Answer [   ]

108 A. Sound waves can neither be seen nor be felt, but the ear is so delicate that it catches all the shades of difference in them.

B. Only when they reach the brain do we hear anything.

C. The hammer, anvil and stirrup of the middle ear take up the vibrations, magnify them, and pass them on through the fluid of the cochlea to the nerve endings of the inner ear and so to the brain.

D. A sound is first caught by that part of the ear that is outside the head and is then sent down the canal to the eardrum, making it vibrate.

Answer ☐

109 A. Dyslexia tends to run in families, and is more common in males than females.

B. Most dyslexics also have problems with spelling.

C. People with dyslexia have trouble seeing the differences between words, and will often misread them.

D. They may reverse the letters in a word, for example substituting 'saw' for 'was', or find substitutes for the printed word, so that 'hot' may be read as 'pot'.

Answer ☐

110 A. The men wore plain linen collars, jerkins and breeches, and had short hair (which earned them the nickname 'Roundheads'), while the women chose dark, plain dress styles.

B. The Royalist side continued to wear elegant court satins, plumed hats and, even for men, long ringlet hairstyles.

C. An important development in the middle of the 17th century was that clothing became an obvious symbol of the religious and political differences that split England during the Civil War.

D. The Parliamentary forces, who were Puritans, adopted very plain clothes.

Answer ☐

Chapter 4
100 English usage questions

Employers are keen on tests of English usage because they want to establish that a candidate can be trusted to produce competent written work. How you use English in business should be, well, business-like, and employers want employees to write letters and e-mails that are clear and to the point. Most will not care if, for example, some punctuation marks are omitted or the finer nuances of grammar are ignored, provided the intended meaning remains unaffected. They want the job done and are unlikely to object unless the errors are serious enough to undermine the confidence of colleagues or customers in the competence of the writer or, worse, damage the image of their organization. They are not usually interested to know if, for example, you use semi-colons correctly (or at all), but they may be reassured to know that you can identify the correct application of the comma, colon and apostrophe.

Few employers' tests of English usage can be described as advanced. They mostly comprise questions at the intermediate level. The majority of candidates will quite quickly be able to revise the rules of usage sufficiently well to pass these tests. Even candidates who have long forgotten the grammar lessons of school or remember them with considerable dread can with sufficient practice master these tests. Once you have revised or learned the rules of usage, these tests will seem far more straightforward. So, practise to revise the rules and you will better realize the principle behind the questions and recognize the significance of the possibly subtle differences between the suggested answers. You will then be well placed to attend on the day, fully prepared to press home your advantage.

Below you will find 100 practice questions presented in the two most common styles of question found in real tests. No time limits are imposed, but if it better suits your circumstances then by all means impose your own time constraint and answer the questions under exam-type conditions. Answers and explanations are provided in Chapter 8.

You will find hundreds more practice questions in the Kogan Page testing titles: *Ultimate Psychometric Tests*, 2008, *How To Pass Graduate Psychometric Tests*, third edition, 2007, and *The Graduate Psychometric Test Workbook*, second edition, 2010.

Correctly complete the sentence

This style of question requires that you select a pair of words from the suggested answers that correctly completes the sentence. You then record the letter that identifies that pair of words in the answer box.

This style of English usage question was once very common; it is now less popular but still in use. Even if you do not face this style of question it is still worth working through them as some important points of usage are revised.

1   Hastings .... developed as a holiday resort after ....

    A. A seaside town
       World War I

    B. a seaside town,
       the first world war

    C. , a seaside town,
       the First World War

    D. , a Seaside Town,
       World War I

Answer

2   When you attend the test centre be sure to bring your personal .... test appointment .... thinking cap.

A. ID, your
   card and your

B. ID your
   card, your

C. ID and your
   card your

D. id, your
   card plus your

   Answer

3   In most tests taken on a computer be sure of your answer before submitting .... go back and review your answer.

A. It, you Cannot

B. it you can

C. it you, can

D. it because you cannot

   Answer

4   The colon is most commonly used to introduce a list: ....
....

A. Paul, John and
   David took pens,
   paper and pencils

B. Pens, paper and pencils
   were all that Paul,
   John and David took

C. Paul, John and
   David took Pens,
   Paper and Pencils

D. pens, paper and pencils
   were all that paul, john
   and david took

   Answer

5   The reason the environmental campaigner dropped his objection to nuclear .... recognized that renewable alternatives .... yet viable.

A. power, he
   where not

B. power he
   were not

C. power: he
   were not

D. power: he
   where not

   Answer

6 The head .... was very surprised to see the .... in the kitchen.

    A. chief   B. chef
       house fly   housefly

    C. chief   D. chef
       house-fly   house fly

                        Answer [   ]

7 The event was .... and the venue less than .... full.

    A. ill-timed   B. ill timed
       three-quarters   three-quarters

    C. illtimed   D. ill-timed
       three quarters   threequarters

                        Answer [   ]

8 She lived on a very busy ...., Farlow ...., and hated the sound of the cars.

    A. Road   B. Road
       Road   road

    C. road   D. road
       road   Road

                        Answer [   ]

9 After a good .... work Peter went to the gym and then for a shower in the .... club.

    A. day   B. day's
       employee's   employees'

    C. days'   D. days
       employees   employee

                        Answer [   ]

10 We will have lunch in .... hour; do you think you will want .... slice of pizza or two?

A. an   B. an
   a   one
C. a   D. a
   one   an

Answer [   ]

11   They spent .... month of June in the French town and
the sun shone almost .... day.

A. the whole   B. all
   every   each
C. all the   D. the all
   every   each

Answer [   ]

12   We were hunting for .... mushrooms but it was so dark
in the wood that we could barely see ....

A. some   B. any
   [no word]   something
C. [no word]   D. some
   anything   some

Answer [   ]

13   .... asked everyone and still haven't discovered ....
cat it is.

A. They've   B. They're
   whose   who's
C. They'll   D. There's
   whose   who's

Answer [   ]

14   The food and drinks manufacturer announced that additives
.... would no longer be .... in any of its products.

A. , including   B. including
   monosodium   monosodium
   glutamate   glutamate
   including   included

C. including
   monosodium
   glutamate
   including

D. , including
   monosodium
   glutamate,
   included

Answer [   ]

15 An object that reflects all parts of the light spectrum except red
        looks .... object that reflects all .... light looks
        white.

A. red, an
   wavelength

B. red while an
   wavelength

C. red an
   wavelengths

D. red, object
   wavelengths

Answer [   ]

16 The painting has taken .... weeks to complete but this is
        a lot .... the last time it was done.

A. less
   less than

B. quite a few
   fewer than

C. quite a few
   less than

D. less
   fewer than

Answer [   ]

17 The exchange rate .... the deal was done was not
        advantageous and consequently the product was not pur-
        chased by members of the social-economic group ....
        it was promoted.

A. at which
   to whom

B. of which
   at which

C. at what
   to who

D. at that
   among whom

Answer [   ]

18   I asked Jim if he was going to the .... you planning
to ....

A. film? Are   B. film, are
   go?   go.

C. film? Are   D. film. Are
   go.   go?

Answer [   ]

19   The newspaper made the .... that it was a ....

A. pre-sumption   B. presumption
   self portrait   self portrait

C. pre-sumption   D. presumption
   self-portrait   self-portrait

Answer [   ]

20   Look at these artichokes: they are the best .... I've seen
but this .... tastes rather bitter.

A. one   B. ones
   [no word]   ones

C. [no word]   D. [no word]
   one   [no word]

Answer [   ]

21   The statement from the solicitor was .... incompre-
hensible and made the judge .... angry.

A. utterly   B. a bit
   dreadfully   totally

C. very   D. extremely
   nearly   completely

Answer [   ]

22   The delay was .... the large number of vehicles and
perhaps another factor was .... the roadworks.

A. owing to
   [no word]

B. because of
   owing to

C. due to
   [no word]

D. because of
   due to

Answer

23   .... he was the cleverest in the family .... at university he failed the most exams.

A. While
   Even if

B. Even if
   while

C. Although
   whilst

D. Where as
   though

Answer

24   By the time the administrator realized her estimate of the
   .... of delegates was wrong it .... too late.

A. number
   was

B. amount
   would have
   been

C. number
   will have
   been

D. amount
   will be

Answer

25   The .... complained that the .... sewing was of
poor quality.

A. bosses'
   seamstress

B. bosss
   seamstresss'

C. bosses
   seamstress's

D. boss's
   seamstres's

Answer

26   He worked hard to improve his .... in Italian but to hear
him speak you would not think he ....

A. proficiently   B. proficiency
   did   did

C. proficiently   D. proficiency
   had   had

Answer [   ]

27 He got up early .... walk the dog and left the house
quietly .... not to wake anyone.

A. in order to   B. to
   in such as way   so as

C. so to   D. so as to
   so   so that

Answer [   ]

28 The problem with the film is that the viewer is ....
provided with all the facts .... told why they should
expect events to unfold as they do.

A. either   B. neither
   nor   or

C. either   D. neither
   or   nor

Answer [   ]

29 Everyone knew the issue was of great .... importance
and the decision would set .... important precedent.

A. [no word]   B. an
   an   a

C. a   D. the
   [no word]   the

Answer [   ]

30 I thought .... left the keys in the car but realized this was
something I .... normally do.

A. its
   won't

B. I'd
   wouldn't

C. I've
   who's

D. I'm
   weren't

Answer [   ]

31 Half the team gave the proposal their .... support while the rest thought it a ....

A. Un-conditional
   nonstarter

B. unconditional
   nonstarter

C. un-conditional
   nonstarter

D. unconditional
   non-starter

Answer [   ]

32 As soon as she finishes her .... assignment she will be let .... on the next one.

A. last
   lose

B. latest
   loose

C. late
   lose

D. later
   loose

Answer [   ]

33 I don't expect to get it back and only placed the advert in the lost and found section of the newspaper as a matter of .... but if anyone calls about the lost money please ....

A. principal
   ask their number
   and I will call back

B. moral correctness
   ask them to call back

C. principal
   ask that they
   call back

D. principle
   take a
   number and I will call back

Answer [   ]

34 Here is the site of the laboratory .... it was invented and it was over there .... the discovery was put to its current day practical application.

A. when
   whose

B. whereby
   where

C. where
   whereby

D. whose
   when

Answer

35 I've always had an admiration .... the work of Willard Van Orman Quine and share with him an interest .... travel.

A. for
   in

B. in
   in

C. in
   with

D. for
   for

Answer

36 The incidence of heart disease .... positively .... the level of salt ingested.

A. correlate
   with

B. correlates
   to

C. correlate
   to

D. correlates
   with

Answer

37 The parliamentary session ended with the Prime Minister refusing to answer the .... was responsible for the release of confidential ....

A. question of
   who
   information.

B. question
   who
   information?

C. question
   information.

D. who
   information?

Answer

38 I .... get the message because it arrived .... I had left for the meeting.

A. did
   no sooner

B. did'nt
   until

C. did not
   after

D. didn't
   before

Answer

39 She told us '......... favourite was .... sausages'.

A. that my
   Frankfurter

B. My
   Frankfurter

C. my
   frankfurter

D. my
   Frankfurter

Answer

40 .... sound broke the silence of the early morning and .... felt like speaking for fear of breaking the magic of the moment.

A. No
   no one

B. Not a
   not any of them

C. Not any
   not anyone

D. None
   nothing

Answer

Identify the correct sentence

The following have been the predominant style of English usage questions. You are required to identify the correct sentence from a series of suggested answers and record in the answer box the letter of the alphabet that corresponds to your selected answer.

41   A. She loved to travel so she could know people from all around the world.

B. She loved to travel so she could get to know people from round the world.

C. She loved to travel so she could knew about people from around the world.

D. She loved to travel so she could get knowing people from round the world.

Answer [   ]

42   A. If it were not for the Prussians Wellington would have lost the battle at Waterloo.

B. If it hadn't been for the Prussians Wellington would have lost the battle at Waterloo.

C. But for the Prussians Wellington would have been lost at Waterloo.

D. If it wasn't for the Prussians Wellington would have lost at Waterloo.

Answer [   ]

43   A. I felt like a drink but I was put off by the male feel of the bar.

B. I wanted a drink but I was put off by the masculine bar.

C. I felt like a drink but I was put off because the bar felt too masculine.

D. I wanted a drink but I was put off by the male bar.

Answer [   ]

44   A. I kept explaining that Oxford is farther than Brighton but she kept asking for further information.

B. I kept explaining that Oxford is farther than Brighton but she kept asking for farther information.

C. I kept explaining that Oxford is further than Brighton but she kept asking for farther information.

D. I walked to the college of farther information but it was further away than I realized.

Answer [   ]

45 A. The ocean depths being recognized as a featureless abyss rather than a dynamic variable and biologically rich environment.

  B. By recognizing the ocean depths as dynamic, variable and biologically rich environment rather than a featureless abyss.

  C. Their recognizing of the ocean depths as a featureless abyss rather than a dynamic, variable and biologically rich environment.

  D. The ocean depths are recognized as a dynamic, variable and biologically rich environment.

  Answer [   ]

46 A. Thank you for bringing me here but let's look at one more picture and then would you please take me home.

  B. Thanks for bringing me here but let's look at one more picture and then would you please bring me home.

  C. Thank you for taking me here but let's look at one more picture and then would you please bring me home.

  D. Thanks for taking me here but let's look at one more picture and then would you please bring me home.

  Answer [   ]

47 A. As soon as he suggested a weekend away she flew up the passage, jumped in the car and sped off down to the country.

  B. As soon as he suggested a weekend away she flew up the passage, jumped in the car and sped off up to the country.

  C. As soon as he suggested a weekend away she flew down the passage, jumped in the car and sped off down to the country.

  D. As soon as he suggested a weekend away she flew down the passage, jumped in the car and sped off up to the country.

  Answer [   ]

48 A. When fishing you can always tell when you lose a fish because the line feels loose.

B. When fishing you can always tell when you loose a fish because the line feels lose.

C. When fishing you can always tell when you loose a fish because the line feels loose.

D. When fishing you can always tell when you lose a fish because the line feels lose.

Answer [   ]

49 A. The milk tasted off and I meant to say something but I did not think of complaining.

B. The milk tasted off and I meant to complain but did not think to say something.

C. The milk tasted off and I meant to complain but decided its not worth it.

D. The milk tasted off and I meant to say something but did not think it worth complaining.

Answer [   ]

50 Which of the following sentences draws a metaphor?

A. Karl Marx labelled the capitalist a parasite on the back of labour because the whole value or produce created by the labouring man belonged to the capitalist.

B. John Locke described how he who gathered the wild fruit, killed, caught or tamed the wild beasts by placing his labour on them acquired a property in them.

C. Adam Smith held that the original state of things which preceded both the appropriation of land and the accumulation of stock were held in common.

D. Galbraith argued for a better balance between private affluence and public poverty, including measures to protect the environment against the excesses of private companies.

Answer [   ]

51   A. I willingly accepted to walk with them over the forest.

   B. I reluctantly agreed to walk with them across the forest.

   C. With hesitation I agreed to walk with them through the forest.

   D. Despite misgivings I accepted to walk with them through the forest.

Answer [   ]

52   A. In the restaurant where I work I get often tips because I always treat well the customers.

   B. In the restaurant where I work I get often tips because I always treat the customers well.

   C. In the restaurant where I work I often get tips because I always treat well the customers.

   D. In the restaurant where I work I often get tips because I always treat the customers well.

Answer [   ]

53   A. When she asked to borrow my computer, I replied yes I'm afraid so.

   B. When she asked to borrow my computer, I replied I'm afraid so.

   C. When she asked to borrow my computer, I replied I'm afraid not.

   D. When she asked to borrow my computer, I replied I'm afraid no.

Answer [   ]

54   A. He had nothing except what he was borne with.

   B. He had nothing apart from what he was born with.

   C. He had nothing besides what he was borne with.

   D. He had nothing apart from what he was borne with.

Answer [   ]

55 A. When the company went bust everyone involved lost all that they had.

   B. When the company went bust everyone involved lost all.

   C. When the company went bust everyone involved lost all what they had.

   D. When the company went bust everyone involved lost what they had.

   Answer [   ]

56 A. After the garage sale the children hadn't hardly any toys left.

   B. After the garage sale the children had scarcely any toys left.

   C. After the garage sail the children had hardly any toys left.

   D. After the garage sale the children hadn't scarcely any toys left.

   Answer [   ]

57 A. I lent my bother's car so I could go for a nice drive.

   B. I borrow my brother's car so I could for a really nice drive.

   C. I lend my brother's car so I could go for the drive of my life.

   D. I borrowed my brother's car and all I did was sit in a traffic jam.

   Answer [   ]

58 A. My eldest daughter was born at 3 o'clock in the afternoon in a cold day in November.

   B. My eldest daughter was born at 3 o'clock in the afternoon on a cold day in November.

   C. My eldest daughter was born on exactly 3 o'clock in the afternoon in November.

   D. My eldest daughter was born on the weekend at 3 o'clock in the afternoon.

   Answer [   ]

59   Which statement has a sarcastic tone?

A. After 20 years the moratorium on hunting whales remains riddled with loopholes that allow whales to be killed and their meat sold as food in the name of science.

B. For many successes there is usually an associated failure. For example, lots of couples rejoice in the fact that their house is worth much more than they paid for it, but they complain that their children can't afford the deposit to buy a home of their own.

C. It is time for religious believers to stand up to secularisms and to defend their faith against progressive policies.

D. He viewed all civil servants as at worst meddling bureaucrats and at best as pointless paper-shufflers.

Answer [   ]

60   A. That particular species of fish is found across the world's oceans and you can identify it from its large colourful spots.

B. That particular species of fish is found over the world's oceans and you can identify it from it's large colourful spots.

C. That particular species of fish is found throughout the world's oceans and you can identify it from its large colour spots.

D. That particular species of fish is found beneath all the world's oceans and you can identify it from it's large colourful spots.

Answer [   ]

61   A. As one gets older one better appreciates life's little comforts.

B. As you gets older one better appreciates life's little comforts.

C. As one gets older you better appreciates life's little comforts.

D. As you gets older you better appreciates life's little comforts.

Answer [   ]

62 A. The police hoped for help in finding the culprit and the missing money from everyone.

B. The police hoped for help from everyone in finding the culprit and the missing money.

C. From everyone the police hoped for help in finding the culprit and the missing money.

D. The police hoped for help in finding the culprit from everyone and the missing money.

Answer [   ]

63 A. Most professional athletes choose this kind of trainers.

B. Most professional athletes choose these kind of trainer.

C. Most professional athletes choose this kind of trainer.

D. Most professional athletes choose these kind of trainers.

Answer [   ]

64 A. He lay between the sheets staring up at the ceiling.

B. He lie between the sheets staring up at the ceiling.

C. He lay among the sheets staring up at the ceiling.

D. He lie among the sheets staring up at the ceiling.

Answer [   ]

65 A. Neither the right wing party or the left wing party is willing to concede defeat.

B. Neither the right wing party or the left wing party am willing to concede defeat.

C. Neither the right wing party nor the left wing party am willing to concede defeat.

D. Neither the right wing party nor the left wing party is willing to concede defeat.

Answer [   ]

66 A. The research found that either obese children must take more exercise or eat less.

B. The research found that obese children must either take more exercise or eat less.

C. The research found that obese children either must take more exercise or eat less.

D. The research found that obese children must take either more exercise or eat less.

Answer

67 A. The papers was requested at the same time as the request was made for the newspaper cuttings.

B. The papers were requested at the same time as the request were made for the newspaper cuttings.

C. The papers was requested at the same time as the request were made for the newspaper cuttings.

D. The papers were requested at the same time as the request was made for the newspaper cuttings.

Answer

68 A. Over the years the trade federation has served its members well.

B. Over the years the trade federation have served it members well.

C. Over the years the trade federation has served their members well.

D. Over the years the trade federation have served its members well.

Answer

69 A. Surprisingly, given the recent profits warning, the chief executive has enjoyed considerable support from they who had previously challenged his leadership.

B. Surprisingly, given the recent profits warning, the chief executive has enjoyed considerable support from them who had previously challenged his leadership.

C. Surprisingly, given the recent profits warning, the chief executive has enjoyed considerable support from he who had previously challenged his leadership.

D. Surprisingly, given the recent profits warning, the chief executive has enjoyed considerable support from those who had previously challenged his leadership.

Answer [   ]

70   A. The fact that the number of humpback whales are increasing prove that the conservation efforts are effective.

B. The fact that the number of humpback whales are increasing proves that the conservation efforts are effective.

C. The fact that the number of humpback whales is increasing proves that the conservation efforts are effective.

D. The fact that the number of humpback whales is increasing prove that the conservation efforts are effective.

Answer [   ]

71   A. If they had not taken so long checking each question before attempting the next question they might not have run out of time.

B. If they had taken so long checking each question before attempting the next question they might not have run out of time.

C. If they had not took so long checking each question before attempting the next question they might not have run out of time.

D. If they had took so long checking each question before attempting the next question they might not have run out of time.

Answer [   ]

72 A. The firm is a major player in the logistics industry to play a significant role in keeping our supermarket shelves well stocked.

B. The firm is a major player in the logistics industry so it plays a significant role in keeping our supermarket shelves well stocked.

C. The firm is a major player in the logistics industry with it playing a significant role in keeping our supermarket shelves well stocked.

D. The firm is a major player in the logistics industry because it plays a significant role in keeping our supermarket shelves well stocked.

Answer [   ]

73 A. I might have paid greater tribute to the contribution of his research assistant had I made the speech at the awards ceremony.

B. I might have paid greater tribute to the contribution of his research assistant if I make the speech at the awards ceremony.

C. I might have paid greater tribute to the contribution of his research assistant if I am making the speech at the awards ceremony.

D. I might have paid greater tribute to the contribution of his research assistant making the speech at the awards ceremony.

Answer [   ]

74 A. The food was cooked to perfection but the portions were too small, also we waited too long between the courses as well.

B. The food was cooked to perfection but the portions were too small and as well we waited too long between the courses.

C. The food was too well cooked and the portions too small, also we waited too long between the courses.

D. The food was overcooked, the portions were small and we waited a long time between the courses too.

Answer [　　　　　]

75 A. The amount of drivers of Ford cars who responded to the survey is as high as it's ever been.

B. The number of drivers of Ford cars who responded to the survey is as high that it's ever been.

C. The amount of drivers of Ford cars who responded to the survey is as high that it's ever been.

D. The number of drivers of Ford cars who responded to the survey is as high as it's ever been.

Answer [　　　　　]

76 A. The class concluded that the exam question was very impossible.

B. The assignment is not very possible.

C. The project was quite impossible.

D. It is widely known that the puzzle is fairly impossible to solve.

Answer [　　　　　]

77 Which sentence includes an example of personification?

A. Nomadic people are the human equivalent of an endangered species and have no defence against the encroachment of loggers and ranchers onto their ancestral lands.

B. Take airline pilots for example; they do not need to attend university to qualify for this job and most pilots are on a salary of $150,000 or more.

C. Recent research provided further stark evidence that in education money still talks, when it was found that bright children from poor homes are failing to get the same grades as bright children from rich households.

D. Planning and then recording in a last will and testament how we would wish our assets dealt with on our death is something more of us should do, and for the majority of us with straightforward affairs a 'do it yourself' will would suffice.

Answer [   ]

78 A. By the time they had completed checking all the forms it will be time to start double-checking them.

B. By the time they had completed checking all the forms it will have been time to start the double-check.

C. By the time they had completed checking all the forms it was time to start the double-check of them.

D. By the time they had completed checking all the forms it was time to start double-checking them.

Answer [   ]

79 A. The girls come to stay alternate weekends and it is so nice to have the family all together.

B. The girls come to stay alternative weekends and it's so nice to have the family all together.

C. The girls come to stay alternative weekends and it is so nice to have the family altogether.

D. The girls come to stay alternate weekends and it is so nice to have the family altogether.

Answer [   ]

80 A. I met a new acquaintance at the club today.

B. I made a new acquaintance at the club today.

C. I meet a new acquaintance at the club today.

D. I came to a new acquaintance at the club today.

Answer [   ]

81   A. Try and eat bread and butter with a fork and knife and you will probably end up on your hands and knees picking it up off the floor.

   B. If you try and eat bread and butter with a knife and fork you are bound to end up on your knees and hands picking it up off the floor.

   C. If you have ever eaten butter and bread with a knife and fork I expect you ended up on your hands and knees picking your food up from the floor.

   D. If you try to eat bread and butter with a knife and fork you are very likely to end up on your hands and knees picking it up off the floor.

   Answer [   ]

82   A. Overall the price increase had the effect of reinforcing the committee members in their determination to increase interest rates.

   B. Overall the price increase had the affect of reinforcing the committee members in its determination to increase interest rates.

   C. Overall the price increase had the affect of reinforcing the committee members in their determination to increase interest rates.

   D. Overall the price increase had the effect of reinforcing the committee members in its determination to increase interest rates.

   Answer [   ]

83   Which sentence suffers most from hyperbole?

   A. Most collectors of postage stamps would give the Earth to own one of the 1920s 24-cent US stamps with an upside-down biplane.

   B. It used to be thought that a diet high in fibre greatly reduced the risk of cancer but it is now thought that eating too much red meat and milk products have a much stronger negative association.

C. There have been many fabulously successful public relations campaigns but when things go wrong they can go spectacularly wrong.

D. We face a pensions crisis because more than half of all working people will rely solely on the state to provide a pension in their old age and the state cannot be trusted to pay it.

Answer [ ]

84 A. As the train moved away from the track the passengers started to jump into the station platform.

B. As the train moved on the track the passengers jumped out of the station platform.

C. As the train moved with the track the passengers jumped out of the station platform.

D. As the train moved along the track the passengers started to jump off on to the station platform.

Answer [ ]

85 Which of the following can you correctly describe as cynical in tone?

A. He wrote saying that he wants to enter the priesthood but I very much doubt that he is serious.

B. The charity raises money to help the homeless but the people working there seem most interested in helping themselves.

C. The election result is a great disappointment.

D. Can you believe it that Frank is going to get married again!

Answer [ ]

86 A. No whales were seen the whole month but ask some expert and they will tell you that they will turn up any time.

   B. Not any whales were seen the whole month but ask any expert and they will tell you they will turn up some time.

   C. No whales were seen the whole month but ask any expert and they will tell you that they will turn up some time.

   D. Not any whales were seen the whole month but ask some expert and they will tell you they could turn up any time.

Answer [   ]

87 A. Mother suggested that the children bring their instruments into the front room but still they played the violins like they were trying to saw them in half.

   B. Mother suggested the children bring their instruments in the front room but still they played the violins as if they were trying to saw them in half.

   C. Mother suggested the children bring their instruments in the front room but still they played the violins like they were trying to saw them in half.

   D. Mother suggested the children bring their instruments into the front room but still they played the violins as if they were trying to saw them in half.

Answer [   ]

88 Which sentence includes a euphemism?

   A. He is difficult to understand when he speaks in that childish voice.

   B. I was really surprised to find out that our house was built over 100 years ago.

   C. A cemetery is a place where people are buried when they pass away.

   D. It is stupid to get annoyed about things that do not really matter.

Answer [   ]

89 A. Foggy though it was the sun still managed to shine through.

B. Foggy as though it was the sun still managed to shine through.

C. Although it was foggy the sun still managed to shine though.

D. Foggy through it was the sun still managed to shine though.

Answer

90 A. The collected datum is proving its possible after all.

B. The collected datum is proving it's possible after all.

C. The collected datum are proving it's possible after all.

D. The collected datum are proving its possible after all.

Answer

91 In which of the following does the verb directly transmit action from the subject to the object?

A. These days the world is run by computers.

B. The world would be a very different place if it were not for computers.

C. A world without computers would be a better place.

D. These days computers run the world.

Answer

92 A. If it would have rained on the last day of the month it would have been the wettest July on record.

B. If it would had rained on the last day of the month it would have been the wettest July on record.

C. Would have it rained on the last day of the month it would have been the wettest July on record.

D. Had it rained on the last day of the month it would have been the wettest July on record.

Answer

93 A. Anyone interested in the reptiles found in Sardinia can learn much if you search on the internet.

B. Anyone interested in the reptiles found in Sardinia can learn much by searches on the internet.

C. Anyone interested in the reptiles found in Sardinia can learn much if they search on the internet.

D. Anyone interested in reptiles found in Sardinia can learn much if she searches on the internet.

Answer [   ]

94 Which of the following statements includes a simile?

A. A red, white and blue flag fluttered.

B. He wandered as if he had all the time in the world.

C. It was a lovely sunny day until the fog rolled in.

D. The shape of the hill was like a fairy cake.

Answer [   ]

95 A. The newspaper reported the football coach as saying that hopefully his team would win.

B. The newspaper reported the football coach as saying that he was full of hope his team would win.

C. The newspaper reported the football coach as saying that he hoped his team would win.

D. The newspaper reported the football coach as saying that he was full of hope his team should win.

Answer [   ]

96 A. He is at a meeting at Newport, the town at the centre of the island.

B. He is in a meeting at Newport, the town in the centre of the island.

C. He is in a meeting at Newport, the town at the centre of the island.

D. He is at a meeting in Newport, the town at the centre of the island.

Answer [   ]

97   A. First I thought I was the only undergraduate at the lecture besides Michele.

B. At first I thought I was the only undergraduate at the lecture beside Michele.

C. At first I thought I was the only undergraduate at the lecture besides Michele.

D. First I thought I was the only undergraduate at the lecture beside Michele.

Answer [   ]

98   A. The criminal recidivist promised to try to change his ways.

B. The reoffending recidivist promised to try and change his ways.

C. The convicted recidivist promised to try to change his ways.

D. The recidivist promised to try and change his ways.

Answer [   ]

99   Which of the following contains a non-sequitur?

A. Most people do not have a sufficient grasp of statistics to tell whether or not the figures produced by their government are correct or being used correctly.

B. Public trust in official data is at an all time low and we can't insist that the general public go back to school and attend classes on the meaning of data and what can be correctly interpreted from it.

C. To produce the official annual inflation rate, government statisticians monitor the price of a basket of 650 goods and services sold at a total of 120,000 outlets.

D. No one can control how statistics are used. Imagine if some statistician were to be made judge in every debate

and intervened to endorse or reject contesting interpretations put onto official figures.

Answer [   ]

100 A. I might have offered the guests a complimentary cup of
coffee if I had been the proprietor of that restaurant.

   B. I might have offered the guests a complimentary cup of
coffee if I had to be the proprietor of that restaurant.

   C. I might have offered the guests a complimentary cup of
coffee if I were the proprietor of that restaurant.

   D. I might have offered the guests a complimentary cup of
coffee if I was the proprietor of that restaurant.

Answer [   ]

Chapter 5
100 True, false or cannot tell questions

This chapter contains 33 passages and 100 warm-up questions for what is fast becoming the most common type of verbal reasoning test question. You are bound to face these reading comprehension and critical reasoning questions at some stage in your career.

Each passage is followed by three questions (the exception is the last passage which is followed by four). Your task is to answer the questions by referring to each passage. You must determine if the correct answer is true, false or that you cannot tell (ie you cannot tell from the information given if the answer is true or false). The questions require you, for example, to comprehend meaning and significance, assess logical strength, identify valid inference, distinguish between a main idea and a subordinate one, recognize the writer's intention and identify a valid summary, interpretation or conclusion.

The subjects of the passage are drawn from a great many fields. It may be current affairs, business, science, the environment, economics, history, meteorology, health or education. In fact, expect almost any subject matter. If you know something of the area then take care not to bring your own knowledge to the passage. You are expected to answer the questions using only the information it contains. Be especially careful if you know a great deal about the subject or if you believe the passage to be factually incorrect or controversial. It is not a test of your general knowledge, your knowledge of the latest findings in the discipline or your political views. So feel at ease about answering true to a statement that is true in the very limited context of the passage but which you know to be false given what you learned at university or read in a newspaper that morning.

When publishers of real tests develop an advanced verbal reasoning test they rely on fine distinctions between the suggested answers in order to distinguish between the scores of the large numbers of candidates. These distinctions are much finer than those we draw on a day-to-day basis. As a result it is common for candidates to feel irritation and complain that these tests are to a large extent arbitrary. In a way they are; after all, this is not how we use language at work or anywhere other than in the surreal world of tests. This is something you just have to accept and get used to and with practice you will get to recognize the subtle distinctions being drawn.

Take care not to err too much towards the 'cannot tell' answer by making the mistake of applying too strict or too inflexible a test of proof. Be sure to read the questions as carefully as you read the passage and learn to pick up the many clues provided in the wording. For example, if the passage refers to 'a valid argument, inference or premise', or asks whether it is necessarily the case that..., then apply a strict criterion of proof. However, if the question asks, for example, is it reasonable... on the balance of probability, that... might the author..., then adjust your criterion accordingly and apply a less strict one. Once again, the only way to master these subtle differences is to practise. You will soon gain more confidence and get better at making the proper judgements.

If, when taking lots of time in the relaxed conditions of your home, you find these questions easy, take care that you do not slip into a false sense of security. In a real test you will be pressed for time and may well be suffering some anxiety. You should aim to undertake just one careful read of the passage and then refer back to it to answer the question. Some people find it helps to read the questions before the passage.

You will find more practice questions at the advanced level in these Kogan Page test titles: *The Graduate Psychometric Workbook*, second edition, 2010, and *How to Pass Graduate Psychometric Tests*, third edition, 2007.

Passage 1

NASA, the US space agency, announced plans to return to the Moon within the next 15 years and this time the plan is to stay. It was 1972 when the last people stepped onto the moon. The next time an astronaut walks there he or she is most likely to visit the polar region rather than the equatorial zone, the site of all previous missions. The poles are the preferred location because they experience more moderate temperatures and are bathed in almost continuous sunlight, which will allow a permanent research station to rely on solar power. Another benefit of the poles regions is that they are believed to hold mineral deposits from which oxygen and hydrogen can be extracted. After a number of robotic scouting missions there would then occur a great many short-duration manned transportation missions. Once operational the station would be permanently occupied with astro-nauts undertaking six monthly tours of duty. They would undertake a wide range of scientific tasks perhaps the most ambitious of which will be to prepare for a journey to the planet Mars.

1   Incredibly, or more likely unintentionally, the passage states that the next astronaut will have to walk to the moon!

   True   False   Cannot tell

                                 Answer [   ]

2   The moon station will operate as a science laboratory and its principal objective will be preparing for a manned mission to Mars.

   True   False   Cannot tell

                                 Answer [   ]

3   The conclusion that the polar region of the moon is the preferred location for the station is wholly dependent on the assumption that the oxygen and hydrogen extracted there could be used by the astronauts.

True   False   Cannot tell

Answer [   ]

Passage 2

Outside the cities, people have no alternative but to drive their cars to get their children to school, get to hospitals and to go shopping. They already pay among the highest petrol duties in the world and an annual road tax that raises far more than is spent on the national infrastructure. Now they face, within a decade, the introduction of road charging, an additional tax that will be charged for each mile travelled. The aim of these additional taxes is to free the roads of traffic, so speeding up businesses and improving the nation's pro-ductivity and efficiency. Then the well off will be able to drive along unencumbered by the mass of ordinary drivers, and the congestion of the rush hour will be a thing of the past.

4   A significant flaw in the case made in the passage would emerge if there were an affordable public transport system serving rural locations.

True   False   Cannot tell

Answer [   ]

5   People living outside the cities already pay a higher rate of duty on petrol than those living in the city.

True   False   Cannot tell

Answer [   ]

6   The rich will be able to drive along unencumbered by the mass of ordinary drivers only if the charges are so high that the majority of road users are priced off the roads.

True   False   Cannot tell

Answer [   ]

Passage 3

Cholera, typhoid, diphtheria and tuberculosis cause huge numbers of deaths. Drinking water has always been the world's greatest single vector of sickness. Disease is transmitted when sewage and drinking water come into contact. Children are particularly vulnerable. In the 19th century half of all children died before the age of 5. In some of the poorest countries the infant mortality rate still stands as high as one in eight. This compares with a rate of 1 in 100 in countries where drinking water is safe. The separation of sewage and the supply of clean drinking water are the domain of civil engineers, and their work makes a significant contribution to public health. That contribution was at last recognized when public sanitation was voted the greatest medical breakthrough, beating discoveries including antibiotics, vaccines and anaesthesia in a poll organized by the *British Medical Journal*.

7   The passage states that cholera is a water-borne disease.

True   False   Cannot tell

Answer [   ]

8   The safe disposal of sewage and the supply of clean drinking water are not medical advances.

True   False   Cannot tell

Answer [   ]

9   The first two sentences are sufficient to draw the conclusion that water-borne disease is still the greatest transmitter of sickness.

True   False   Cannot tell

Answer [   ]

Passage 4

'End the external consultant's gravy train' was the message from the cross-party accounts committee of the Houses of Parliament. The use of consultants in the public sector has soared over the past three years to the point where members of the committee considered it to have reached an expensive, unproductive dependency. The evidence they heard left them unable to establish the benefit of the practice, and they voiced deep concerns about the lack of performance reviews in most contracts. They were also critical of the failure of management to support in-house tenders submitted by departments' own teams. The view of the committee was that these bids represented far greater value for money when compared to the companies that were awarded the work and who charged rates as high as £2,000 a day. It was also felt that savings could be made if, instead of payment on the time taken, consultants were engaged on price paid for the work done.

10   A gravy train is a situation where someone can easily make a lot of money.

   True   False   Cannot tell

                                           Answer [   ]

11   The passage states findings of an investigation by the committee into the benefits of using consultants in the private sector.

   True   False   Cannot tell

                                           Answer [   ]

12   Billions have been wasted on consultants over the three years.

   True   False   Cannot tell

                                           Answer [   ]

Passage 5

People should buy more fresh food to use in preparing proper meals. What is more, they should whenever possible buy locally produced food from local shops. Instead, we treat food like fuel: we seek out the cheapest and most convenient, which is often processed industrially and supplied by multinationals, which has consequences for both public health and the environment. We eat it in a hurry and on the move rather than eating together around a table. Many meals contain too much fat and sugar, giving rise to obesity and high blood pressure; pre-packed meals are expensive and wasteful because of all the packaging and distribution involved. People just do not respect food enough and largely lack the skills and knowledge needed to turn back to good food.

13 The author's attitude towards junk food is ambivalent.

True   False   Cannot tell

Answer

14 It can be inferred from the passage that pre-packed meals are cheaper than fresh food.

True   False   Cannot tell

Answer

15 The author would probably consider the fact that people do not have time to appreciate food, buy it locally, prepare and cook it themselves and eat it together, as illustrative of his argument.

True   False   Cannot tell

Answer

Passage 6

Road signs and traffic lights at junctions and busy crossing points may be removed in order to improve road safety. The idea may seem contradictory and goes against the decades-long trend of separating and controlling traffic and pedestrians. The idea is to create anxiety, principally in the mind of the driver, so that he or she slows down and pays greater attention. Current demarcations between pavement and road will be made indistinct by removing railings and kerbs, resurfacing both in the same material, and re-laying them so that they are on the same level. Neither drivers nor pedestrians will then feel they have right of way and both, as a consequence, will behave more cautiously. When a driver reaches a junction at which there are no traffic lights he or she must take responsibility for deciding when it is safe to cross. Previously the driver relied on the traffic lights to decide his or her action and this created a dangerous state of denial of accountability. Incredibly, the initiative is claimed to not only make the streets safer but also to reduce congestion.

16   Leaving aside the issue of safety, an explanation of the ultimate sentence in the passage would be 'Traffic moves more naturally and there are no more unnecessary delays at red lights when no other vehicle is in the vicinity.'

   True   False   Cannot tell

                                             Answer [   ]

17   If you observe a junction where the lights are out there is rarely congestion.

   True   False   Cannot tell

                                             Answer [   ]

18   The principal case made in the passage can be summed up as 'Removing lights removes barriers to traffic flow and improves behaviour and safety.'

   True   False   Cannot tell

                                             Answer [   ]

Passage 7

Particles were collected in blocks of a silicon-type material called Aerogel as a space probe passed through the tail of a comet at the very edge of our solar system. Incredibly the probe then returned to Earth and scientists were able to use spectrometers and electron microscopes to identify the mineral and chemical compositions of the particles. The probe travelled almost 3 billion miles and passed within 150 miles of the comet at great speed. At that point the Aerogel was exposed and particles from the comet's tail that struck it were slowed down and stopped by the gel-like material, trapping them. The Aerogel and its unique cargo then began the three-year journey back to Earth. Some of the particles are believed to pre-date the sun and to have remained unchanged in very cold deep space for all of their existence. Importantly, the sample was considered free of contaminants derived from the great planets of our solar system and the asteroid belt.

19 Among the finds were particles that pre-dated our solar system that had not changed since their creation.

True   False   Cannot tell

Answer

20 According to the passage, the findings have startled scientists.

True   False   Cannot tell

Answer

21 The claim that the particles were too small to reveal their mineral content can be rebutted by the content of the passage.

True   False   Cannot tell

Answer

Passage 8

A survey of how children spend their pocket money found that a sizable amount of it is spent on sweets, snacks and fizzy drinks. The study was based on 4,000 children who were asked to keep a diary of their purchases over a two-year period. On average the children spent $23 a week and over a third of this was spent on sugary and fatty food and drinks. The survey found marked differences in spending trends in sex and age. Boys spent less on clothes, shoes and toiletries and more on games, computer-related items and hobbies. The biggest spenders were children aged 13 to 15 years. The children spent equal sums on mobile phones and charges, and activities and objects that could be classed as educational. Both sexes spent equal amounts on music, but boys spent more on sporting activities.

22 The survey probably confirms many parents' worst fears.

   True   False   Cannot tell

                                      Answer [   ]

23 The survey found that boys devote a greater part of their non-food spending on sporting activities than girls.

   True   False   Cannot tell

                                      Answer [   ]

24 The passage does not allow the reader to infer the amount children spend on books.

   True   False   Cannot tell

                                      Answer [   ]

Passage 9

Workers now caught by the top rate of income tax include university lecturers, mid-ranking civil servants and officers of local authorities, specialist nurses and sisters, police inspectors and senior officers in the ambulance and fire service. This trend means that an extra 3.5 million workers are liable for the higher rate of tax compared to 10 years ago. More than 1 million extra people pay tax at the higher rate because growth in pay has increased faster than inflation-linked tax allowances. Over the period, these allowances have been increased in line with or less than inflation, while wages have increased at a rate of more than inflation. As a result, every year more people find themselves taxed at the highest rate for the first time. The Treasury defends the trend on the basis that the increase in numbers is a result of rising incomes and living standards. Critics point out that the higher rate of tax begins at a far lower point than in other countries. In Spain, the highest rate of tax is not applied until income is 2.5 times the average wage, while in the UK the highest rate is paid by anyone who earns 1.3 times the average wage.

25   The trend to which the passage refers is of wages increasing at a rate higher than inflation.

True   False   Cannot tell

Answer

26   Linking tax allowances to inflation has caused over 3 million people to pay the higher rate of tax.

True   False   Cannot tell

Answer

27   The cause of the increase can correctly be summarized as growth in pay having outstripped inflation-linked tax allowances, so the number of people paying tax at the highest rate has increased.

True   False   Cannot tell

Answer

Passage 10

Intellectual property is little more than the right to extract payment when our cultural outpourings should be free to share. In the digital world we are all authors, publishers and critics, so why should some be allowed to lay claim to our common cultural heritage and expression and enjoy the recognition of paternity? Why should the corporate media conglomerates be allowed to use copyright, patents and intellectual property laws to make criminals of thousands of users of virtual communities if they share music videos and written works? These users freely share their own work, and if all work were to be donated in this way the public sphere would be transformed into a more cultural, creative place.

28   The author of the passage would agree that the people who write books, poems, plays and film scripts, even though they may have taken years to write them, should donate the product of their craft for free.

True   False   Cannot tell

                                    Answer [   ]

29   The passage does not present an either/or scenario but allows for a balance to be struck.

True   False   Cannot tell

                                    Answer [   ]

30   The word 'paternity' in the context of the passage means 'fatherhood'.

True   False   Cannot tell

                                    Answer [   ]

Passage 11

Our international institutions and treaties have failed to move with the times. They were formed to provide mechanisms through which to confront common threats while protecting national interests. But interdependence and interconnectedness have advanced beyond anything imagined at that time and the global institutions have proved utterly impotent at providing effective global governance. On the one hand we have a fast emerging global economy and a spectrum of global communities but on the other no effective global governance. All too often efforts to address the many common challenges are pulled down by narrow national interest. Collectively we have proved incapable of protecting the environment from the damage wreaked by individual companies and nations. Those institutions have proved powerless. The world lacks and increasingly needs mechanisms capable of protecting the collective.

31 The author believes that the world needs a new system of global stewardship.

True   False   Cannot tell

Answer [   ]

32 It can be inferred from the passage that we are in the middle of a global revolution.

True   False   Cannot tell

Answer [   ]

33 The passage is correctly classified as an example of the liberal school of political thinking. This school of thought argues that the interests of the nation state must be protected and the individual must be protected from the excesses of government.

True   False   Cannot tell

Answer [   ]

Passage 12

The Environmental Commissioner of the European Commission wants to introduce tough new limits for the emissions of carbon dioxide for all new vehicles. She wants mandatory maximum levels of emissions for all new cars by 2012. Manufacturers are lobbying against a mandatory limit and prefer a voluntary target for average emissions that is lowered annually, year on year. The luxury brand manufacturers are lobbying hardest, as they consider a mandatory limit to represent the greatest threat to their operations. The Industrial Commissioner has proposed a compromise that favours voluntary targets but will also commit manufacturers to realizing improvements in tyre performance, the introduction of emission-reducing speed management systems, and greener manufacturing and recycling of vehicles. European car makers believe that many jobs will be lost if the Environmental Commissioner gets her way. The 20 Commissioners who make up the Commission will have to decide.

34   The author sees the issue as a test of the Commission's green credentials.

   True   False   Cannot tell

                                   Answer [   ]

35   Members of the Commission are split over the decision.

   True   False   Cannot tell

                                   Answer [   ]

36   The passage contains a tautology.

   True   False   Cannot tell

                                   Answer [   ]

Passage 13

So many people ask why children aren't taught grammar and punctuation at school. Many of our teachers today have been produced by the same education system that they now teach in, so the simple answer is that they can't teach grammar and punctuation because they have never learnt it themselves. There have in recent years been meaningful improvements in the level of functional literacy among school leavers, but at the other end of the spectrum universities are complaining about the poor writing skills of undergraduates. These complaints are not raised because of a failure by students to correctly use the subjective clause or to err by leaving participles dangling, but far more fundamental failures in, for example, the use of apostrophes and capitalization. Most commentators describe errors of grammar and punctuation as irritating. To become irritated one must first recognize the error, and the majority of people, including many teachers, do not have a sufficient grasp of the rules to realize that a mistake has been made.

37   Most people don't object to bad grammar and punctuation.

True   False   Cannot tell

Answer [   ]

38   You can infer from the passage that you can only break a rule of grammar if you know the rule in the first place.

True   False   Cannot tell

Answer [   ]

39   The author would agree that bad grammar might be an irritant for a small number of purists but otherwise it does not matter.

True   False   Cannot tell

Answer [   ]

Passage 14

El Niño, the cyclic warming of the Pacific Ocean, is largely responsible for the recent worldwide period of higher than average temperatures. February was the sixth warmest since records began in 1880, but January's record high means that the two-month period was the warmest worldwide. The averages were obtained by combining land and ocean surface temperatures. The only exceptions were areas of the Middle East and central areas of the United States, which did not experience record temperatures. Some of the largest temperature increases occurred in high latitudes around the Artic Circle, where wildlife has responded to the early spring-like weather. Should March not follow the trend and a wintry spell return, some of the species that have woken early from hibernation or started breeding prematurely may experience problems.

40 The passage can be correctly summarized as describing the world's two warmest winter months since records began.

True   False   Cannot tell

Answer [   ]

41 China did not experience record temperatures.

True   False   Cannot tell

Answer [   ]

42 If the average had been based only on land temperatures rather than land *and* ocean temperatures, the result would have been cooler.

True   False   Cannot tell

Answer [   ]

Passage 15

The Bank of England Monetary Policy Committee is discussing the next shift in interest rates. A month ago, every commentator would have predicted an increase, but since then two big trends have emerged, one international the other national, and no one now expects a rise. Instead the talk is of cuts, but for the time being anyway it is probably too early to say when a cut might be made. There has been a series of downbeat figures across the Eurozone. Italy and the Netherlands are officially in recession and manufacturing figures for Germany are in contraction. The French economy may be even weaker than generally perceived. As far as the UK is concerned, figures for the retail and housing sector suggest they have both slowed and demand for manufactured goods is following the global decline. Meanwhile, the price of services has risen above the level of inflation and in line with rising wage costs.

43 The international trend referred to in the passage relates to disappointing data from Europe.

True   False   Cannot tell

Answer [   ]

44 The national context has recently become one in which there is very little pressure for an interest rate rise.

True   False   Cannot tell

Answer [   ]

45 It can be concluded from the passage that the Bank of England Monetary Policy Committee will cut interest rates soon.

True   False   Cannot tell

Answer [   ]

Passage 16

Children as young as 4 will qualify for summer schools, Saturday morning school and online tuition under a scheme to track the brightest of children through school and on to university. The scheme is a major extension of the national gifted and talented agenda to address the fact that mixed-ability teaching has failed to challenge the brightest. 'Gifted' refers to children of high intelligence, while 'talented' is applied to children with an exceptional ability in a specific discipline. In every school a teacher will be made responsible for identifying beneficiaries and they will rely on their peers, assessments and national Key Stage tests. However, teachers tend to recommend children who produce good work on paper and who behave themselves rather than the really gifted and talented. This means that, for example, the child whose high intelligence makes him or her a bit of a misfit is overlooked.

46   Children not labelled as gifted may well feel like failures.

   True   False   Cannot tell

                                   Answer [   ]

47   Gifted and talented children will be identified by their peers.

   True   False   Cannot tell

                                   Answer [   ]

48   A reason given for the initiative is that gifted or talented children may not always behave themselves.

   True   False   Cannot tell

                                   Answer [   ]

Passage 17

Scandinavia is an egalitarian delight if compared to Greece on the division of domestic labour between the sexes. Greek men were the least reconstructed in Europe, but almost as bad are the Czechs, where just 2 per cent of men admit to ironing their own clothes and only 5 per cent claim to do any cleaning in their homes. Men are slightly better represented in the kitchens of northern Europe, with one in five men claiming to be mainly responsible for cooking, but less than 10 per cent in the southern states. For cleaning their homes, the top men are from Latvia and Demark, who are twice as likely to clean as their Spanish counterparts.

49   An important flaw in the case made would emerge if it were discovered that women want equality at home as well as in work.

   True   False   Cannot tell

                                   Answer [   ]

50 The primary purpose of the passage is to promote equality of the sexes.

True   False   Cannot tell

Answer [   ]

51 It is possible that women living in the south of Europe do not expect men to share responsibility for the family, while their northern counterparts do.

True   False   Cannot tell

Answer [   ]

Passage 18

The hippocampus region of the brain usually starts to shrink when we reach the age of 30. This contraction is held to be responsible for age-related memory loss, and the older we get the worse it becomes. The process may be reversible though, as the hippocampus is the only region of the brain in which neurons can grow. New research suggests that the secret to growing them is physical exercise, which raises the possibility of us working out to boost our brainpower. Unfortunately, it is not just any sort of exercise that stimulates the growth of neurons and this explains why physically active people suffer the same memory loss as the more sedentary.

52 The passage states researchers have identified the forms of physical exercise that stimulate the growth of neurons in the hippocampus.

True   False   Cannot tell

Answer [   ]

53 The intended audience of the passage is the physically inactive rather than the general population.

True   False   Cannot tell

Answer [   ]

54   By saying that contraction of the hippocampus is held to be responsible, the author indicates that there may be disagreement on the point.

True   False   Cannot tell

Answer [   ]

Passage 19

According to the 'best MBA annual survey', The Lynx Business School has been the best in the world for the last three years. Four of the best five schools are based in the United States; the only non-US school in the top five is the Glasgow Business School. Stanford and Harvard were in second and third place respectively. In seventh place, up three from the last survey, came the University of the North West. Currently in nineteenth place is the Bombay School, the highest ranked business school outside of the United States and Europe.

55   The Lynx Business School is based in the United States.

True   False   Cannot tell

Answer [   ]

56   The Glasgow Business School came fifth in the survey.

True   False   Cannot tell

Answer [   ]

57   By 'best' the author of the survey most likely means the school voted by a panel of experts to be the pre-eminent.

True   False   Cannot tell

Answer [   ]

Passage 20

The number of very young children with diabetes has risen dramatically in the past 20 years. The number of children under 5 who have the type 1 form of the condition has increased fivefold. This dramatic increase is either the symptom of a marked improvement in diagnosis, or because more genetically susceptible children are surviving birth and infancy, or it suggests that the environment in which we raise our children has become more dangerous for their future health. The exact cause is unknown, but it is believed to be at least in part inherited. The chances of a child developing type 1 diabetes remains low, but the recent increase is too great to be explained by genetic factors alone. It may be that we are exposing our children to something new and that is the cause, or that we have reduced exposure to something that was preventing it previously.

58   It is reasonable to conclude from the passage that five times as many children develop diabetes now than did 20 years ago.

   True   False   Cannot tell

                                  Answer [   ]

59   If the cause is environmental, then the author would agree that we must be exposing our children to something new and dangerous to their health.

   True   False   Cannot tell

                                  Answer [   ]

60   A plausible explanation of the increase could be that the principal age at which the condition is diagnosed has become lower.

   True   False   Cannot tell

                                  Answer [   ]

Passage 21

In Italy, there are about 17 mosquito species and six genera. Mosquitoes there are associated with every type of water body and include species with narrow and broad environmental requirements. They can be grouped according to oviposition site (water or land), overwintering stage (egg, larva or female), preferred host (mammals, birds or amphibians) and number of generations per year (one or many).

61 Would the following fact weaken the case made in the passage: no species of mosquito is found in brackish water?

True   False   Cannot tell

Answer

62 'Genera' is a plural word meaning 'a class of things'.

True   False   Cannot tell

Answer

63 It can it be concluded from the information provided that all the species of mosquito need both aquatic and terrestrial environments during their life cycle.

True   False   Cannot tell

Answer

Passage 22

An atlas that is attributed to Christopher Saxton and printed around 1580 includes the earliest known printed plan of a city in the modern-day United States. Christopher Saxton was born an Englishman, in fact a Yorkshire man. His atlas contains five coloured charts created by the cartographer Giovanni Battista. They illustrate a survey of England and Wales, and the expedition of Sir Francis Drake to the West Indies and what is now the United States. For many generations the atlas formed part of the library of Sherburne Castle in Oxfordshire.

64 The volume contains the first printed map of England and Wales.

True   False   Cannot tell

Answer ⌷

65 By stating that the atlas is attributed to Christopher Saxton, the author is hinting that it may in fact not be his work.

True   False   Cannot tell

Answer ⌷

66 You can infer from the passage that the atlas was multifunctional.

True   False   Cannot tell

Answer ⌷

Passage 23

Alcohol and tobacco are more harmful than illegal drugs such as cannabis and ecstasy, according to a new system that ranks drugs according to the estimated harm they cause. The system rates alcohol as only slightly less harmful than drugs such as heroin and cocaine. Tobacco appears in tenth place in the league table of 20 substances, well above the ranking of many illegal substances. Social harm, including crime, the cost to the state, and illnesses associated with a substance's use and whether or not it could be taken intravenously were considered in deciding the ranking. Alcohol and tobacco are responsible for 90 per cent of drug-related deaths in countries in which their use is legal.

67 You can infer from the passage that alcohol and tobacco's rating reflects their prevalence.

True   False   Cannot tell

Answer ⌷

68   The main point made in the passage is that legal drugs cause more harm than illegal ones.

True   False   Cannot tell

Answer _____

69   Under the new system, cannabis is ranked in the lower half of the table of substances.

True   False   Cannot tell

Answer _____

Passage 24

Opponents complained that the decision was designed to socially engineer by discriminating against middle-class students. The chair of the Leader Teachers' Association had grave concerns over the change. Mr Langham said that it would encourage children to lie about their origins, and asked who is going to establish the veracity of the disclosures. Landowners could describe themselves as farmers, wealthy people who retire early could describe themselves as unemployed. The university admissions service has announced that information on the occupation, education and ethnicity of the parents of applicants will be made available to admissions officers. In the past this information was held back until after places were offered.

70   For the first time admissions officers will know if the parents of people applying to their university also went to university.

True   False   Cannot tell

Answer _____

71   You can infer from the passage that only middle-class applicants will be required to disclose this information.

True   False   Cannot tell

Answer _____

72 A synonym of 'veracity' is 'misconduct'.

True   False   Cannot tell

Answer [   ]

Passage 25

Under section 36 of the Trade Descriptions Act 1968, goods are deemed to have been manufactured or produced in the country in which they last underwent a treatment or process resulting in a substantial change. Meat from animals coming into the UK and then cured here can be described as UK produce. Most well-known brands of ham or bacon are often advertised with packaging depicting a British countryside scene and described as 'farmhouse', which would lead shoppers to believe they are buying products made from British meat, but most are in fact made using imported meat.

73 The author of the passage believes that the practice risks some consumers being duped.

True   False   Cannot tell

Answer [   ]

74 Under section 36 of the Act, British lamb exported to France and slaughtered there is sold as French.

True   False   Cannot tell

Answer [   ]

75 The passage leads the reader to agree that the practice of importing foods and then processing them so that they are substantially changed should be stopped.

True   False   Cannot tell

Answer [   ]

Passage 26

If you choose to go to the theatre, stay in a hotel or catch a plane at one of the more popular times, it is usual for you to be charged the highest price. An influential report recently suggested that this principle should be extended to other activities, including essentials such as transport. If its recommendations were to be implemented, it would mean that we would be charged even higher fares on, for example, trains during the rush hour. It would also mean that we would be charged more to drive our cars at peak times. The level of charge suggested would have the effect of forcing many drivers off the road at these times.

76 At peak times drivers could avoid paying the highest band of charge by switching to public transport.

True   False   Cannot tell

Answer [   ]

77 You can infer from the passage that, to work, the proposal would require a charge for both the number of miles travelled and the time of the journey.

True   False   Cannot tell

Answer [   ]

78 The comparison made in the passage between the theatre and travel is flawed, because travellers who could not switch their journey to off-peak times would have no alternative but to pay more. You can choose to go to the theatre or stay in a hotel on a particular day, and if funds are short then you can take up the offer of a lower tariff at less popular times, or give up on the treat altogether. This flaw means that the proposed charges will fail to reduce congestion at peak times.

True   False   Cannot tell

Answer [   ]

Passage 27

What determines whether a product will succeed or fail? In 1990, six out of ten new products lasted for less than three months in the marketplace. In 2007, two out of ten succeeded. These products are all promoted and great emphasis is placed on brand and logo. Still, most fail and manufacturers must go a bit further if they are to improve the prospects of their product's success. Your iPod (you almost certainly have one) does not have a logo on it but it is instantly recognizable from its shape and feel. What about your mobile phone? There is a good chance it is a Nokia, and when it rings you immediately recognize the tone, which is a part of the Nokia brand. An incredible 60 per cent of people recognize it.

79 Given that the world's population is around 8 billion people, you can infer from the passage that exactly 5 billion people will recognize the Nokia ringtone.

True   False   Cannot tell

Answer [   ]

80 The author's strategy is to look at success stories.

True   False   Cannot tell

Answer [   ]

81 The passage is making the point that product success depends on more than a catchy brand name and a memorable logo.

True   False   Cannot tell

Answer [   ]

Passage 28

An old adage in economics was that 'When the United States sneezes the rest of the world catches a cold.' In the first half of 2007, growth in the United States slowed, while over the same period growth in the Eurozone accelerated and growth in Japan almost doubled. It still is true that the Central Southern American and Canadian economies remain susceptible to the importation of recession from the United States. But the spillover of a US recession to the rest of the world seems less likely these days because the US economy no longer has the same clout as it used to have.

82 The author would not agree that the US economy accounts for roughly the same proportion of global activity as it did 30 years ago.

True   False   Cannot tell

Answer [   ]

83 It seems we can conclude from the passage that we no longer have to look across the Atlantic or Pacific and panic every time the US cyclical activity takes a turn for the worse.

True   False   Cannot tell

Answer [   ]

84 The fact that the 2001 US recession was accompanied by a sharp slowdown in the rest of the world, while the 1982 US recession was not widely reflected, can be taken to be evidence in support of the hypothesis offered in the passage.

True   False   Cannot tell

Answer [   ]

Passage 29

March is a transitional month and can bring snow or warm weather. Last week saw balmy weather that ended with a bitter snap. No lasting damage was done and the trees and bushes that had shown the first sign of green and blossom bounced back. Spring flowers had appeared, and daffodils, hyacinths and primroses were an incredible sight in gardens and parks. The freeze put the burst of spring flowers on temporary hold.

85 The freeze lasted the whole of last week.

True   False   Cannot tell

                                                    Answer [   ]

86 You can't tell if it snowed this March, but from the passage you can infer that it would be unusual if it did.

True   False   Cannot tell

                                                    Answer [   ]

87 The warm weather triggered an early burst of spring flowers.

True   False   Cannot tell

                                                    Answer [   ]

Passage 30

The problem is not so great with hydroelectric schemes in temperate regions. But, before more hydropower schemes are built in tropical zones, the United Nations wants experts to examine the emissions produced by existing schemes and to recommend ways in which they can be made more environmentally friendly. A lot of the tropical hydropower plants were created by flooding forests, and as drowned plants and trees rot millions of tons of greenhouse gases are released. Despite burning no fossil fuels, the greenhouse emissions from these hydropower plants are higher than comparable fossil fuel-burning power plants. The most polluting hydropower installations are those that were created by the flooding of vast areas of carbon-rich land. These are usually shallow reservoirs, and over the first 10 years of their life it is estimated that they generate four times more greenhouse gases than equivalent modern coal-burning power stations to produce the same power output.

88   The problem is not so great from hydroelectric schemes in temperate regions because the cooler temperatures mean that much less greenhouse gases are produced.

True   False   Cannot tell

Answer [   ]

89   You can infer that the United Nations does not think that using the movement of flowing water to drive turbines to generate electricity is necessarily a green source, even though it does not burn fossil fuels.

True   False   Cannot tell

Answer [   ]

90   The greenhouse gas that is largely responsible for the problem is methane, produced as the lush vegetation flooded by tropical reservoirs rots.

True   False   Cannot tell

Answer [   ]

Passage 31

Even when policies seem gender-neutral they can still affect men and women differently. Soon laws will mean that all public bodies in every area, from health and education to transport, will have a new responsibility to demonstrate that they are treating men and women equally. The law is outcome-focused rather than process-driven. The test of fairness will be the measurement of the experience of men and women and the amount of progress towards stated improvements. The new duty will ensure that men and women are treated and targeted equally.

91   The new law might mean that a supermarket must change the way it advertises so that men or women respond equally to promotions.

True   False   Cannot tell

Answer [   ]

92   It can be inferred from the passage that seemingly gender-neutral policies may affect men and women differently because men and women often have different needs.

True   False   Cannot tell

Answer [   ]

93   The main idea of the passage is that the new law should be outcome-focused.

True   False   Cannot tell

Answer [   ]

Passage 32

A massive increase in the amount of spam occurred last year, and spammers have moved from trying to sell fake medicines and counterfeit goods to what are called 'pump and dump' shares. It seems incredible, but spam-filtering companies report that the increase led to the amount of spam doubling, to the point where 19 out of 20 e-mails were unsolicited. This is not a claim to dismiss easily as an exaggeration, as it comes from the company responsible for filtering a quarter of all the world's e-mail traffic. The pump and dump shares are what are called 'penny shares' that the spammers promote through 100 million e-mails (a quarter of all spam), claiming that the price is about to increase rapidly. They only achieve a very low hit rate, but because they send out so many e-mails, enough people buy the shares that the price does rocket and the spammer is able to sell at a massive profit.

94   The intention of the author is to warn the reader that the very large rise in spam is coming from tricksters.

True   False   Cannot tell

Answer [   ]

95 A subordinate claim in the passage is that all unsolicited e-mail traffic is spam.

True   False   Cannot tell

                                       Answer [   ]

96 The author finds it hard to believe that the problem got so bad that only 5 per cent of e-mails were solicited.

True   False   Cannot tell

                                       Answer [   ]

Passage 33

A study that followed the health of 420,000 people who had used a mobile phone for an average of eight and a half years, in an effort to investigate the common fear of a link between their use and cancer, has published its findings. Some of the group had used a mobile since they were first introduced 20 years ago, and fears of a link have persisted throughout that period. If such a risk did exist, even a small one, then given the very widespread use of mobile phones it could cause thousands of additional tumours. Anecdotal evidence and smaller earlier studies had suggested a higher rate of brain and neck cancer among phone users. The very large number of subjects in this study and the long period over which it was conducted mean we can have great confidence in the result. The study expected 15,000 tumours to occur in the sample population for the period, and a figure higher than this would suggest a link between the use of mobile phones and the risk of cancer.

97 The study found a small link between the use of mobile phones and the risk of cancer.

True   False   Cannot tell

                                       Answer [   ]

98 You can correctly infer from the passage that the study involving 420,000 subjects is the most authoritative review yet of a link between cancer and the use of mobile phones.

True   False   Cannot tell

Answer [   ]

99 After 20 years, scientists should at last be able to state with confidence whether or not mobile phones cause cancer.

True   False   Cannot tell

Answer [   ]

100 If true, the fact that more than 15,000 tumours occurred in the sample would weaken the conclusion of the passage.

True   False   Cannot tell

Answer [   ]

Chapter 6
Decision analysis

These tests are about making good judgements in less than ideal circumstances – as is often the case in real life. The information provided is deliberately incomplete and the rules being followed are deliberately ambiguous. It is your task to decipher the code and then – despite the fact that the information is incomplete and that there is uncertainty – decide which of the suggested answers are best. You have to do this within a tight time frame.

This chapter comprises 35 practice questions. You are provided with a short description of a situation, as well as a list of codes and their corresponding meanings. The situation and codes are followed by questions and each question involves a sequence of codes and a series of suggested answers. In some instances more than one suggested answer is correct. It is your task to identify which of the suggested answers are the best interpretation of the code, given the context and the given meaning of the codes. Note that the sequence of codes can be used in a different order from that in which they are presented in the question. So, for example, the code xx (meaning rock) and yy (meaning paper) can be used to correctly construct the interpretation rock, paper or paper, rock. Also note that other words (not covered by the code and not contradicted by the context) can be added to the suggested answer and it can still be correct. For example, it would be correct to translate the code xx, yy as rock and paper, paper or rock and so on. Pay particular attention to the commas in the questions. If two codes are not separated by a comma then they relate to each other and only each other. If the codes are separated by commas then they may relate to any of the other codes in the given sequence. You are expected to answer the questions using only the information provided, so be especially careful to stick to the content of the situation. In many of the questions below, you can select the answer or reject suggested answers depending on the information provided in the context.

Decision analysis questions

Read the situation and answer the 15 questions that follow it, deciding which in your opinion is the best suggested answer or answers. Note that the first 10 examples have one best answer and the last 5 more than one best answer. Be sure to consider that your answer applies the code sequence correctly *and* is consistent with the situation.

Situation 1

A courageous group of citizens at great personal risk formed a secret order, the aim of which is to campaign by peaceful means for reform of the great divide between the rich and poor in their society. They champion the poor and the disenfranchised and highlight the inadequate public infrastructure such as the bad schools to which the poor must send their children and the polluting industries in which they work. They argued for the introduction of welfare programmes and the modernization of industry. They propose the redistribution of wealth by taxing the rich and thus raising the funds needed to fund their reforms. Most of their members are imprisoned and continue their work using coded messages passed to the outside world by sympathetic prison staff. You work for an international human rights group which decodes their messages and publishes them on the internet. Use the matrix to identify in your judgement the best interpretations of the code sequences.

<u>Codes</u>

Converters

81. Equivalent	84. Decrease
82. Enlarge	85. Similar
83. Turn around	

Key terms

221. Wrong	229. Public
222. Reform	230. Better
223. Industry	231. Must
224. Children	232. Pollution
225. Rich	233. Education
226. High	234. Vote
227. Result	235. Accept
228. Poverty	236. Merit

Select only one best answer to the first 10 questions.

Q1   234, 231, 83 225, 83 221

    A. The poor must never be given the right to vote.

    B. The rich must give the poor the right to vote.

    C. The poor must struggle for the right to vote.

    D. How can it be right that the poor cannot vote?

                                      Answer [   ]

Q2   81 236, 224, 230, 233

    A. Our children deserve a better education.

    B. The children of the disadvantaged crave to be educated.

    C. All children irrespective of their background value a good education.

    D. Education should only be for the children of the better off.

                                        Answer [   ]

Q3   231, 226, 235, 225

    A. There is no reason why the rich must accept such high levels of taxation.

    B. We must accept that the rich will not accept our proposals.

    C. The rich must be forced to accept our proposal for high taxation.

    D. We must convince the rich to accept that high taxation is in their interest too.

Answer [   ]

Q4   223, 231, 232, 85 222, 85 83 226

    A. Pollution is the unavoidable consequence of the drive for greater productivity in industry.

    B. Pollution must be stopped through the transformation of industry.

    C. Industry must be modernized to lower pollution.

    D. Dirty industries must be closed to counter pollution.

Answer [   ]

Q5   221, 85 228, 229, 85 225

    A. Wealth alongside public squalor is wrong.

    B. Public displays of affluence are wrong when there are shortages.

    C. It is naive to say that public affluence is wrong when there is squalor.

    D. If I were poor I would feel wronged by public displays of wealth.

Answer [   ]

Q6   82 222, 84 230, 231

    A. Revolution would be OK but it must be peaceful.

    B. Change by any reasonable means is acceptable.

C. Change by any means possible must be more tolerable to the status quo.

D. Civil disobedience as a means to an end must be all right.

Answer [   ]

Q7 228, 232, 83 227

A. Pollution is the foundation of poverty.

B. Inequality is the cause of poverty and pollution.

C. Poverty is the basis of pollution.

D. Poverty and pollution are unconnected.

Answer [   ]

Q8 233, 224, 83 221, 85 230

A. It is mistaken to believe that all children benefit from education.

B. A good education is the right of every child.

C. A good education for a few gifted children is superior to a poor schooling for every child.

D. All children have a right to a good education.

Answer [   ]

Q9 225, 232, 81 230, 85 83 226

A. The rich suffer from the effects of high pollution as well.

B. Improve pollution and the rich benefit too.

C. Lower pollution is healthier for the rich too.

D. The rich are worse placed to avoid the consequences of pollution.

Answer [   ]

Q10 225, 83 225, 231, 230

A. Rich and poor must work for the better.

B. For the better of society the rich must stay rich.

C. We can only achieve our goals if the rich and the poor work much better together.

D. The rich must always be regarded as better than the poor.

Answer [   ]

The next five question have more than one 'best' answer.

Q11 85 231, 228, 235

A. We should accept the necessity of poverty.

B. We ought not to accept that people have to live in poverty.

C. In such a rich country we are not obliged to accept that people must live in poverty.

D. It is a fact that poverty can be abolished and we should work to achieve it.

Answer [   ]

Q12 224, 221, 233, 83 225

A. It's wrong that some children receive a poor education.

B. It's wrong that underprivileged children receive a poor education.

C. Deprived children should at least receive a good education.

D. It's wrong that poor children are deprived of a good education.

Answer [   ]

Q13 226, 85 229, 222

A. Unrestricted taxation is necessary if we are to reform our community.

B. The planned reform of the civic sphere necessitates high taxation.

C. High taxation is needed if we are to reform our community.

D. The reform of the system of taxation will fund the proposed welfare programmes.

Answer [   ]

Q14 81 236, 222, 223

    A. Many plus points will result from the reform of industry.

    B. The reform of industry will bring many advantages.

    C. Industry badly needs reform and it will bring great value.

    D. There is great worth in the wish to reform industry.

Answer   [   ]

Q15 222, 223, 235, 232, 85 234

    A. Mark your ballot for reform and stop pollution from industry.

    B. The choice is reform industry or accept pollution.

    C. Accept only change vote for the reform of industry and the abolition of pollution.

    D. Don't accept pollution and reform industry by putting your cross on the ballot paper.

Answer   [   ]

End of test.

Four decision analysis mini-tests

Working quickly is especially important in the decision analysis sub-tests and so I have organized the rest of the practice in this section as mini tests. We can all get most of these questions right if we take lots of time over them but in a real decision analysis test you are pressed for time and may well be suffering from some anxiety. Be sure to practise decoding the question quickly and correctly and making a fast, accurate decision. That way you will correctly complete more questions in the time allowed and consequently achieve a higher score.

Each mini-test contains five multiple-choice decision analysis questions and you are allowed five minutes in which to attempt all five. The first question is of average difficulty and they become progressively harder. You are told in every instance when you are required to identify more than one best answer. If there is no instruction to identify more than one best answer, identify one of the suggested answers as best.

Get the most out of this practice by setting yourself the personal challenge of trying to beat or, if you get all five right, match your last score each time you take a mini-test. That way you will create a realistic, real-test feel. You will need to try very hard and take the challenge seriously if you are to really succeed in beating your previous best score or getting five out of five every time. Time management will be critical, so be sure to stick to the four-minute time limit and not spend too long on any one question, and practise making one careful, detailed read of the passage to save on time going back to check detail. Keep practising until you consistently get all five questions right. Achieve this and you can take strength from the fact that you are likely to make a very good start in a real decision analysis paper. The only thing then left to do is to keep up that rate of success through to the end of the real test!

Mini-test 1

Situation

Philately attracts both collectors and investors and has performed well, beating the return on most of the rest of the economy. Some of the best returns have been realized on examples of otherwise everyday stamps that carry even very small differences. Investors dominate this part of the market and compete fiercely to acquire examples of some of the world's most rare and valuable stamps. The market makers are constantly alert to the infrequent occasions when examples come up for sale.

You work for a leading dealer and are preparing for the auction of a unique British stamp dating from the 1920s on which the king's head appears upside down. You must decide which of the suggested answers are, in your best judgement, the correct interpretation of the following five sequences of code.

Note: unless otherwise stated, each question has only one best answer.

Codes

Modifiers

99. Expand

100. Reduce

101. Reverse

102. Similar to

Terms

222. Makes
223. Unique
224. Buy
225. Small
226. Feature
227. Price
228. Twenty
229. Cheap at
230. Collectors

231. Smith
232. Million
233. Stamp
234. Sold
235. Jones
236. Investment
237. Any
238. Bid
239. Years

Q1 224, 237, 102 227

A. It is worth any price.

B. Buy at any cost.

C. Buy no matter the consequences.

D. Buy any of them no matter the outlay.

Answer [   ]

Q2 232, 228, 231, 238

A. Smith will bid to 20 million.

B. We already have an offer of 20 million from Smith.

C. Expect the bids to go way beyond 20 million.

D. Smith bid 20 million.

Answer [   ]

Q3 102 224, 236, 233. Identify more than one of the suggested answers as 'best'.

A. An investor will most likely buy the stamp.

B. The stamp will be acquired for a collection.

C. The stamp will be bought as an investment.

D. He plans to purchase the stamp as an investment.

Answer

Q4   228, 239, 99 232, 234, 233

A. Twenty years ago an identical stamp sold for millions.

B. Countless collectors would give 20 years of their life to own such a stamp.

C. Twenty millions are too much for a stamp so it will not be sold for years.

D. This stamp is the most exciting thing for 20 years and will be sold for millions.

Answer

Q5   226, 233, 229, 223, 101 102 225, 227

A. The unique upside-down head is an eye-catching feature and makes this stamp worth every cent of its anticipated high price.

B. The unique feature of the stamp is striking and makes it cheap at any price.

C. This stamp is titanic and its unique feature makes it cheap at the price.

D. The unique, conspicuous feature of this stamp makes it cheap whatever the price.

Answer

End of test.

Mini-test 2

Situation

Home-completed assignments contribute between 20 and 60 per cent of the marks to many national examinations. Most students believe such assignments are a fairer method of assessment compared with 'all or nothing' exams. Many educationalists are opposed to home-completed assignments because they are so difficult to invigilate. A confidential survey found that cheating was widespread and that the situation had become much worse due to plagiarizing from the internet. Use the matrix to identify the best interpretations of the findings and conclusions of the survey.

Codes

Transformers
01. Like   03. Inflate
02. Nothing like   04. Trim down

Dictionary
101. Help   110. Model
102. Easy   111. Siblings
103. Admit   112. All
104. Children   113. Do
105. Cheat   114. Offer
106. Grade   115. Students
107. Websites   116. Increase
108. Parents   117. Big
109. Assignments

Q1   103, 104, 108, 109. Note: more than one of the suggested answers is 'best'.

A. Parents admit to doing assignments for their children.

B. Assignments are often completed by the parents and not the children.

C. Children admit that parents sometimes do the assignments for them.

D. Children admit that their parents help with the assignments.

Answer [   ]

Q2 02 117, 107, 110, 114

A. For a fee websites offer full-length model essays.

B. For a small fee websites offer model answers to assignments.

C. Perfect 'A Star' grade assignments can be bought off the internet.

D. Examples of faultless assignments can be bought for a modest fee from a whole host of websites.

Answer [   ]

Q3 115, 01 103, 102, 105

A. Students declare that it does not matter if it is easy to cheat because no one does.

B. Students who cheat are encouraged to come clean and admit what they have done.

C. Students like to say that they cheat but most do not because they are too afraid of the consequences if they are caught.

D. Students confess that it is all too easy to cheat.

Answer [   ]

Q4 02 115, 115, 101

A. Students complain that teachers help them too much.

B. Some learners receive so much help that it is not possible to say that the work is entirely theirs.

C. Teachers have been caught giving students too much help.

D. In some cases it is not entirely their own work because learners have received too much help.

Answer [   ]

Q5 111, 101, 106, 108, 01 116

A. Inappropriate help from parents and siblings has led to grade inflation.

B. Parents and siblings have helped boost the grade awarded.

C. Parents and siblings help students get a higher grade than they otherwise would.

D. Cases of enlarged grades have resulted from the help provided by parents and siblings.

Answer [   ]

End of test.

Mini-test 3

Situation

To make his lazy relatives work for their inheritance an agoraphobic and severely moral billionaire buried a horde of precious jewels and metals in a secret location. He confided in no one and left the following coded clues and a set of street maps of most of the world's capital cities as directions to the treasure. The family have been looking ever since and have assembled the following suggested answers to the encoded clues. Use your best judgement to decide which of the suggested answers is the most likely best interpretation.

Codes

Modifiers

55. Join
56. Similar to
57. Turn around

58. Equivalent to
59. Type of

Lexis

30. Circle
29. Wood
28. Stop
27. Treasure
26. Fish
20. Mountain
19. City

25. Cow
24. Me
23. Look
22. Flat
21. Card game
16. Rock
15. Three

18. Broken   14. Under

17. Dig   13. Primitive plant

Q1 27, 55 29 16, 56 24

    A. I buried the treasure in a rocky outcrop above the tree line.

    B. You'll find the treasure in a wooden box covered with rock.

    C. The treasure is in an abandoned coal mine.

    D. Dig for my treasure where the rocks stand as tall as trees.

                              Answer [   ]

Q2 28, 15, 59 21

    A. Stop at the town with three casinos.

    B. Stop by the three men playing a game of cards.

    C. Play three hands of poker and then stop.

    D. Stop by the bridge with three spans.

                              Answer [   ]

Q3 16, 23, 58 22. Note that more than one of the suggested answers should be judged as best.

    A. From the top of the jagged rock look west.

    B. Look for a place where the rock is smooth.

    C. Find the flat rock and look carefully.

    D. Look in the apartment for a piece of rock.

                              Answer [   ]

Q4 56 29, 56 30, 58 18 16

    A. You will find it in the wooden hold of the sunken wreck on the reef.

    B. Lift the planks and find the ring of stones.

    C. You will find it in the tree that has grown around the rock.

    D. Find the old pump in the timber yard and slowly move the handle up and down.

                              Answer [   ]

Q5   57 20, 55 13 25, 19

A. Take a plane to Moscow.

B. You can see the city from the hilltop.

C. It's a frighteningly steep valley where dense rainforest covers the ancient city.

D. It was placed in the ground near a flat patch where the animals graze.

Answer [   ]

End of test.

Mini-test 4

Situation

The secret of the ultimate paper plane made from a single sheet of A4 paper and not involving any cuts or the addition of anything such as sticky tape, glue or weights is a closely guarded secret. The indoor world flight record for such a plane when launched at a height of 2 metres is in excess of 20 seconds over a distance of 60 metres. The keys to the ultimate design are a snub nose and delta wings. To discover more of the secrets on how to build a record-beating paper plane of your own, decipher the following codes and identify the suggested answer that represents the best interpretation of them.

Codes

Transformers
999. Akin to   997. Equivalent of
998. Expand

Vocabulary
100. Tape   91. Nose
99. Increase   90. Folds
98. Design   89. Slant
97. Stable   88. Choice

96. Minimize

95. Important

94. Flight

93. Drag

92. Upwards

87. Wing or wings

86. Lift

85. Construct

84. Strength

Q1   94, 91, 97

A. A pointed nose is superior to a blunt one because it ensures more stable flight.

B. A blunt nose ensures a more stable flight than a sharp one.

C. A pointed nose ensures the flight is more stable than a snub one.

D. A blunt nose is better than a pointed one because it ensures more stable flight.

Answer [   ]

Q2   98, 85, 999 88. Note that more than one of the suggested answers are 'best'.

A. The best designs are uncomplicated to construct.

B. Choose a design that is straightforward to construct.

C. Design a plane that is easy to construct.

D. Select a delta wing design that is simple to construct.

Answer [   ]

Q3   90, 100, 84, 96, 93

A. Folds are used to give strength and if you tape over them you minimize drag.

B. Maximize the strength of your design by using folds and tape to impart strength and minimize drag.

C. Minimize drag and use folds but not tape to impart strength.

D. While folds give strength minimize the number so as to reduce drag.

Answer [   ]

Q4   999 89, 86, 99, 87, 92. Note that more than one answer is the 'best'.

   A. Incline the wings upwards to increase lift.

   B. Increase the wing size to produce more upwards lift.

   C. Lift the wings upwards to increase the camber.

   D. Adjust the wing to increase the lift.

Answer [   ]

Q5   998 95, 98, 87, 91

   A. Fundamental to the design is the choice of the nose and wing.

   B. The design of the nose and wings is vital.

   C. Significant features of the design are the nose and wings.

   D. The wings are more central to the design than the nose.

Answer [   ]

End of test.

Chapter 7
Four timed realistic tests with interpretations of your score

This chapter provides four practice tests designed so that you may develop a good exam technique and improve your stamina and endurance under test conditions.

In each test the time allowed, number and level of difficulty of the questions, and the competencies tested are similar to real tests used by employers. Undertake these tests under conditions as realistic as possible by finding yourself a quiet place where you will be able to work for the suggested time limit without interruption. Approach each test as if it were the real thing and be sure that you apply the sheer hard work and continuous concentration essential for a good score in a real test. Practise the effective management of your time and remember not to spend too long on any one question.

To create a truly realistic test experience, set yourself the personal challenge of trying to beat your last score each time you take one of these practice tests. You will need to try really hard and take the challenge seriously if you are to realize this aim.

After each test review your answers and go over the explanations to any questions that you got wrong. You should aim to understand better the gaps in your knowledge, and before you take the next test, set about further practice of the sort found in earlier chapters with the intention of reviewing the principles you do not fully understand. Use the interpretation of your score to determine the amount and type of practice you still need.

Test 1   Sentence sequence

You are allowed 25 minutes to complete this test, which comprises 40 questions. Each question comprises four sentences. The sentences are identified by the letters A to D, but the order in which they were originally written has been lost and most of the sentences are now in the wrong order. Your task is to put the sentences into the correct or original order.

Record your answer by placing the letters in the answer box in the order in which you think they were originally.

Set a watch or stopwatch function on, for example, a mobile phone to the time allowed. Work where you will be free of distractions and complete the test in one sitting.

1   A. A professional homeopath, as a result of education, training and clinical experience, is competent to treat patients presenting with a wide variety of conditions.

    B. No one system can deal with all that an individual may need, or serve the entire population.

    C. Homeopathy may not always be the most appropriate form of treatment.

    D. Homeopathy is a unique system and therapeutic discipline that fulfils an important role in healthcare; it serves to prevent ill-health as well as being of benefit to most patients with both acute and chronic diseases.

Answer [   ]

2   A. If, however, there is an opposing piece in the next black square, and an empty black square beyond it, then that piece may be captured and removed from the board by jumping over it.

   B. Black always has the first move.

   C. Sometimes several pieces can be taken like this in a single row and the winner is the player who either captures all his or her opponent's pieces or blocks them so that they cannot move.

   D. A move is made by advancing a piece diagonally forward into an empty black square touching the one it is currently in.

Answer [   ]

3   A. In those days shields were very large, and rose at the middle into two peaks with a hollow between them, so that Thafta, seen far off in the sea, with its two chief mountain peaks and a cloven valley between them, looked exactly like a shield.

   B. Long ago in the small and mountainous island of Thafta lived a king named Umonico.

   C. The country was so rough that people kept no horses, but there were plenty of cattle.

   D. People used to say that Thafta 'lay like a shield upon the sea', which sounds as though it was a very flat country.

Answer [   ]

4   A. Once you've sat down somewhere inconvenient, do not spring up just because you've been asked politely.

   B. The quickest way to do this is to park on a double yellow line, which is the daily street protest undertaken by most city dwellers.

   C. To start this, you need to park yourself somewhere where the police will have to move you on.

D. Civil disobedience is a legal requirement of any demonstration.

Answer [   ]

5   A. The range, manufactured by electronics giant Gizmo, comprises an internet-enabled washing machine, micro-wave oven and air conditioning unit, as well as the first 'smart fridge', which has an internet connection and the capacity to form the hub of a future home network.

B. The technology involved is already available to consumers.

C. Home networking, as it's called, connects every appliance in the home, from your PC to your central heating, via a central hub, which can then be accessed and controlled via the internet.

D. Indeed, one company has already launched the first range of such appliances in the UK.

Answer [   ]

6   A. The Trojans gathered on a height in the plain, and Hector, shining in armour, went here and there, in front and rear, like a star that now gleams forth and now is hidden in a cloud.

B. With dawn Agamemnon awoke, and fear had gone out of his heart.

C. Then a great black cloud spread over the sky, and red was the rain that fell from it.

D. He put on his armour, and arrayed the chiefs on foot in front of their chariots, and behind them came the spearmen, with the bowmen and slingers on the wings of the army.

Answer [   ]

7   A. At 3,560 feet, Snowdon is the highest mountain south of the Scottish Highlands.

B. Its 845 square miles make only a slightly smaller area than the 866 square miles of the English Lake District.

C. Snowdonia is the second largest national park in Great Britain.

D. Over 500,000 people climb it each year.

Answer [   ]

8 A. They may seem like an arcane field of investigation: after all, are there not more pressing problems with extant species?

B. But the development of a species, its transformations and final extinction are all elements that can be applied to current-day biology.

C. Their closest living relative is the horseshoe crab.

D. Trilobites roamed the world's oceans some 500 million years ago.

Answer [   ]

9 A. The huge amount of energy is radiated out from the core and some eventually reaches Earth, keeping us alive.

B. It has been doing this for 4,500 million years, but is still only halfway through its lifetime.

C. The sun is using up its mass at the rate of 4 million tonnes each second!

D. It is a middle-aged star.

Answer [   ]

10 A. The same applies to spacecraft that operate in places where there is no atmosphere at all.

B. Jet airliners fly at heights of 10,000 metres or more.

C. Such aircraft are said to be pressurized.

D. At such heights the atmosphere is so thin that the aircraft must have its own air supply with oxygen at the normal pressure.

Answer [   ]

11   A. This is usually caused by a reaction to pollen, and is therefore particularly common when flowers are open.

   B. The eyes may be affected in the same way, becoming itchy, sore and weepy.

   C. Many people suffer from hay fever.

   D. The lining of the nasal cavity becomes sensitive and inflamed and produces a large amount of mucus, so the nose runs and the person sneezes a lot.

   Answer

12   A. Particular finger positions or gestures of the hand, common to their age and civilization, delivered a message that was instantly recognized by those who understood the symbolism.

   B. Since ancient times hands have been used in cave paintings, drawings, sculpture and fine art as symbols of communication.

   C. European religious paintings represented the Holy Trinity by the extended thumb, index and middle fingers of a hand.

   D. Ancient Egyptian and Semitic art, for example, depicted celestial power by a hand painted in the sky.

   Answer

13   A. Without food, small birds can quickly starve to death.

   B. Somehow they must maintain reserves at a level that allows them to avoid both starvation and predation.

   C. Too little fat and they may starve to death, while too much increases the energy required for flight, causing them to be slower, less agile and more at risk of predation.

   D. To survive a long, cold night or periods during the day without eating, birds need to put on fat reserves.

   Answer

14   A. The sapwood is less dense and therefore softer than the heartwood.

   B. The heartwood is extremely dense and hard and its only job is to support the tree.

   C. It is therefore much wetter than the heartwood.

   D. It provides support too, but it also carries water and mineral salts (sap) up the trunk.

   Answer [   ]

15   A. A series of islands or chains in the head or heart lines may point to an imbalance of the biochemistry due to mineral deficiencies.

   B. It follows that any impairment of the lines reveals that the constitution is somehow weakened.

   C. Clear, strong lines in the hand are thought to reflect robust health.

   D. A similar effect on the life line reveals poor vitality and a weakened constitution.

   Answer [   ]

16   A. Its plan to increase the amount of municipal waste we recycle to 33 per cent by 2015 has been described as 'depressingly unambitious' by a parliamentary committee, as most Western nations have already surpassed this level.

   B. In parts of Belgium, for example, 72 per cent of biodegradable waste is recycled or composted, compared with about 11 per cent in the UK.

   C. The government has been criticized for its laissez-faire attitude.

   D. While other countries are well on their way to meeting the EU levels by recycling and composting, the UK is lagging far behind.

   Answer [   ]

17   A. The attacks are often brought on by pollen or dust, or occasionally by some kind of food to which the person is allergic.

   B. This makes it difficult to breathe and the person wheezes.

   C. Asthma is serious.

   D. The muscles in the walls of the bronchioles contract, so the tubes get narrower.

Answer [   ]

18   A. A 20-year study has found that taking 300–400 micrograms a day of this B-vitamin can cut your risk by 20 per cent.

   B. Folic acid, long recommended to women trying to conceive, could prevent strokes too.

   C. It helps break down homocysteine, an amino acid that occurs naturally in the body and has been linked to artery-wall damage.

   D. Folic acid is found in broccoli, tomatoes, kidney beans, liver, some citrus fruits and leafy green vegetables such as spinach, or is available in pill form.

Answer [   ]

19   A. If enlargement of the EU goes ahead, it will increase by 10 member states by the beginning of 2004.

   B. When these countries attain membership, hundreds of thousands will want to move to the West in search of higher incomes and, in time, as citizens of the EU, they will be perfectly entitled to do so.

   C. Arguably the most important fact about immigration is that in the next two decades much of it will be lawful.

   D. Much of the small print remains to be agreed, but it is likely that the EU will increase by 30 per cent.

Answer [   ]

20   A. Under the plan the group would sell its private equity division to its management, who would then manage the $2 billion of investments owned by the group.

B. The decision has forced the group to consider selling its own private equity operation in order to avoid a conflict of interest.

C. The move would see Axis surrender control of its equity investments in favour of funds managed externally.

D. Axis is preparing to invest $650 million in Ava Investors, the Orlando-based private equity firm set up to manage the wealth of the billionaire Savini family.

Answer

21   A. Latuga's banks have lent £100 million at an annual negative interest rate of 1 per cent.

B. This means that instead of Latuga paying interest on the loan, the banks will pay Latuga £1 million a year in interest.

C. Latuga, the world's biggest producer of tinned greens, turned the banking world on its head by taking out the first ever negative interest loan.

D. The banks were happy to agree the loan because it has allowed them to acquire bonds and shares, which are forecast to grow by as much as 5 per cent a year.

Answer

22   A. The arts in the UK must to an observer seem to be booming, with new galleries opening in the capital to great acclaim, thriving regional institutions, and ambitious plans to open a major centre of contemporary art in the North West.

B. Add to this the fact that three years ago the Chancellor gave the arts a considerable financial boost, and the National Lottery Fund has provided millions of pounds of lottery money to pay for new venues or renovating existing ones.

C. Yet the Arts Council expresses fears that even after such record spending, some arts institutions are struggling to survive and risk financial collapse.

D. There is some evidence to support this surprising view if one compares the funding for museums and galleries per capita across Europe, for then one realizes that the UK continues to lag behind its neighbours in arts expenditure.

Answer [   ]

23 A. But if the government does about the nation's diet and level of exercise what it has done about most health risks such as smoking and drinking alcohol, which is very little or nothing, then the level of obesity will continue to rise and the health of the nation will continue to fall.

B. In the face of such likely government inaction, the only real alternative engines for change are education and litigation, but unlike smoking and drinking there is nothing intrinsically unhealthy about eating, so it is hard to imagine how recourse to the courts could force change on the nation's eating habits.

C. That leaves education, and given that fast-food chains and sugar drink companies have a massive presence in almost every campus, state school and even hospital, it is hard to imagine how the cash-starved educational institutions can alone counter the junk food movement.

D. If the government is willing to regulate to force disclosure of the content of what we eat, get junk food out of schools, make available more healthy alternatives, and install bike racks in public places to encourage more exercise, then the health of the nation will improve.

Answer [   ]

24 A. Some economists have been expressing fears for a considerable length of time about an unsustainable boom that could turn into a bust.

B. The admission comes in a report to the Home Affairs Committee setting out the implications of the continued rise, fuelled by low unemployment, low interest rates and a shortage of housing stock.

C. In a startling reversal the government has acknowledged that house price inflation is a significant problem rather than just an issue.

D. The report identified that the issue became a problem for first-time buyers in London and the South East, and for professionals who could not afford to live in this region, so creating shortages of essential workers in hospitals, schools and the Civil Service.

Answer [   ]

25 A. This time a synchronized recession took place whereby all the major economies slowed down and took with them many others, including Argentina, Mexico, Singapore and Taiwan.

B. The IT and telecommunications-driven fall in investment expenditure began in the United States and spread to the world's other economies, leading to worldwide economic recession.

C. The bursting of the hi-tech bubble is the most important reason for the slowing growth, but it has been made worse by the fact that each of the major economies has its own home-grown problems, which exacerbated the downturn.

D. In the two previous economic downturns, one or more of the biggest economies has been able to avoid recession.

Answer [   ]

26 A. Fay travelled to the same destination by train third class, with her battered suitcase and few possessions; she hoped to find work teaching English but when the war intervened she volunteered to work in a Red Cross hospital.

B. The two women were to meet in the great city under the most unlikely circumstances.

C. Her family had fallen out of the middle class into poverty, and her marriage to a second-rate musician had ended sterile and pointless, but she looked forward to a new life with courage and enthusiasm.

D. Lorenza went to Roma in a chauffeur-driven limousine; she was the daughter of a Venetian aristocrat whose family boasted two Doges from the 17th century, and her life to that point had been typical of her class, with high society parties and travel.

Answer [   ]

27   A. First, our economy is driven by expenditure on luxury goods, and because they are luxury they are non-essential and so can be avoided altogether if the price becomes too great or the spare cash we have in our pocket each month becomes too little.

B. Second, the potential housing bubble and the difficulty being experienced by public sector workers struggling to afford a home is peculiar to the South East, so why apply a general interest rate increase in an effort to address a regional problem?

C. I would argue that interest rates should be left unchanged, and nothing be done to the rate in order to tackle a housing problem that is not creating general inflationary pressure.

D. The property boom and the profits people are making from it may be the only thing preventing our economy sliding into recession, so why risk it?

Answer [   ]

28   A. Hard on her heels is the US Deputy Secretary of State, who is expected to emphasize the fact that they also expect a crackdown on its most polluting industries as a matter

of urgency in order to ensure that the entry conditions to the treaty are realized.

B. In the diplomatic game of grandmother's footsteps, in which the world powers try to coax China to sign the environmental treaty, they seem to have forced the Beijing authorities to realize that they must take the first half step.

C. If the authorities fail to control the level of emissions they are vulnerable to the unfair charge that corruption is preventing action; this, on top of the threatened diplomatic and economic isolation, is thought to be sufficient to ensure China will become both a signatory and a compliant member within the next three years.

D. Today the President of the European Union will deliver to the Chinese authorities the uncompromising message, endorsed by the Union Member States, that failure to follow words with actions could lead to diplomatic isolation.

Answer [   ]

29 A. The areas of the country identified with the worst problems were mainly located in the South East of the country, along with North Yorkshire and the Lake District.

B. It comes on the day a senior minister called for 100,000 new homes a year to be built in villages and hamlets to create and sustain populations large enough to support rural shops and schools.

C. The need for more and better homes was reported to be most acute in the social housing sector, yet that sector was dwindling as tenants exercised the right to buy in areas of high demand, where thousands of people on low incomes or living on benefits are priced out of the property market.

D. The need for more social housing is outlined in a stark report from the Countryside Agency, the government's main adviser on rural issues, which was published today.

Answer [   ]

30 A. The commission also wants insurers to be legally bound to provide compulsory cover for pedestrians and cyclists involved in accidents with cars.

   B. A shake up of the law governing the industry across Europe will make it far easier for individuals to switch insurance companies.

   C. Plans were announced by the European Commission that should lead to greater competition in the vehicle insurance market.

   D. It should mean that companies are no longer able to restrict the length of time motorists may keep their vehicles in EU states other than the ones in which they are registered.

   Answer [   ]

31 A. The Commission is drawing up a dossier of information to demonstrate to the Home Office that women are being unfairly excluded from the force and that the test has very little bearing on the work of the police.

   B. The Commission argues that a police officer very rarely has to run down the street after a criminal, and so whether or not they can run fast or have a firm grip is irrelevant to the job and prevents many able female applicants from becoming officers.

   C. The present test involves an endurance run and upper body and hand strength tests, which the Commission would like to see replaced with a health screening.

   D. The Equality Commission is pressing the Home Office to change the fitness test used for the recruitment of police officers, which it is argued is unfairly biased towards male applicants.

   Answer [   ]

32 A. The study found that 70 per cent of children reported that their dreams reflected their viewing habits, while only 60 per cent of adults reported that television influenced their dreams.

B. Research has found that children's dreams are influenced more by television than adults', while adults' dreams are affected most by what they are reading.

C. Fantasy books were linked to a higher rate of nightmares amongst both children and adults, with children, for example, reporting that scary books caused nightmares.

D. The analysis found apparent links between respondents' dreams and the subject of their reading.

Answer

33 A. Sunday's vote is expected to be noticeable in one other respect, as the socialist vote stood firm while generally the left vote collapsed.

B. Sunday's vote places in perspective some of the more excitable commentary in the United States on France becoming a fascist state.

C. On Sunday, when the second round of the French parliamentary elections is completed, it is likely that the country will have a president and parliament of the same political persuasion for the first time for a number of years.

D. The far-right vote also collapsed because of the centre right's tougher policies on crime and immigration, and because of the poor standard of the right-wing candidates, many of whom hardly bothered to campaign.

Answer

34 A. Epidemiologists know that the virus is by far the leading cause of human disease worldwide, infecting virtually all children before the age of 5.

B. Fortunately, research has established much and the investigation has led to the trial of a vaccine, with promising results.

C. Unlike bacteria that spread via contaminated water, meaning that people in the poorest parts of the world suffer disproportionately, the pathogen is found to be responsible for the same level of incidence of disease in advanced nations such as the United States as in poor regions, including the Asian subcontinent.

D. The virus's ubiquity is due to it being highly contagious and this means it is transmitted irrespective of sanitation.

Answer [   ]

35 A. The proportion of over-50s using the internet to shop, chat, pursue hobbies and study has doubled.

B. Eleven per cent of the over-50s population said that they have sold something over the internet, while one in four have bought something over the net in the past six months.

C. However, a significant number of older people risk being left behind as the digital divide grows.

D. Older people had been slow to adopt the technology but are now fast catching up; however, a significant minority remain offline despite the falling cost of the technology. Those on the lowest incomes and with the fewest qualifications are most likely to miss out on the digital revolution.

Answer [   ]

36 A. The bullet-like silver digital radio is a great compact unit and is powered by two AA batteries, which provide around 20 hours of power, or through an in-car power jack point.

B. The unit has a backlit LED screen and produces really good sound with great bass depth, the screen is easy to read and the unit can switch between mono and stereo mode.

C. When travelling by car, reception quality is unfortunately intermittent especially when in built-up areas, so a regular but quick shift along the frequency bands is necessary to solve the problem.

D. More expensive than other units, the quality and features put it ahead.

Answer [   ]

37 A. The cells used would have to achieve the US Department of Energy's standard of 10 per cent water-splitting efficiency before the investment would be worthwhile and the output would approach the 10 litres level.

B. If the rooftops of every house in the United States were covered in these cells, every household would have at its disposal the hydrogen equivalent of over 10 litres of petrol (gasoline) a day.

C. There is much talk of a hydrogen economy, and one version of that future is described as based on dissociating water into hydrogen and oxygen, using sunlight in photo-catalyst cells or films.

D. But this kind of efficiency has only been achieved under careful laboratory conditions using ultraviolet light. Sunlight comprises only 4 per cent ultraviolet light, so the search is still on for a photo-catalyst that reaches the same level of efficiency using the whole sunlight spectrum.

Answer

38 A. I came to this proposition circuitously while studying chimpanzees and then orang-utans for over 17 years in their natural habitats.

B. My proposition is not incompatible with the dominant view but it adds a role for a cultural input into the evolution of intelligence for all social species, whereas previous explanations saw a cultural input as uniquely human.

C. A human child learns primarily from its parents and from the social and wider cultural context in which that family group lives; this also applies to the offspring of the great apes.

D. The most influential explanation of intelligence is that it evolves in animals that live socially, as it allows them to form the most advantageous relationships and to react quickly to changes in social situations.

Answer

39 A. The fourth assessment of global warming stated that it is unequivocal, will go on for centuries and very likely is man-made.

B. The third assessment was produced in 2001 and stated that most of the warming over the past 50 years is likely to be due to the increase in greenhouse gas concentrations.

C. In 1995 the third report concluded that the balance of evidence suggests a discernible human influence on global climate.

D. And the first report in 1990, by comparison, asserted that warming is broadly consistent with current climate change models.

Answer [   ]

40 A. The player must follow a fast-moving dance routine while standing on an interactive mat that feeds their movements back into the console.

B. One hundred US children, all the offspring of public employees, received as a gift from their parents' health insurance provider, a free dance game and console.

C. The insurance provider hopes that the results will be positive and as a consequence they will pay out fewer claims linked to the treatment of diseases triggered by obesity.

D. The initiative is part of a study to see if such games can reduce the levels of obesity suffered by more than a third of public employees' children.

Answer [   ]

End of test.

Test 2 Word swap

This test comprises 40 questions. Allow yourself eight minutes to complete it.

Each question comprises a sentence in which two words have been swapped. What this means is that one word has been put in the place of another and that word has been put in the original word's place. No other words have been moved. Your task is to identify these two words and record them in the answer box. Be sure that you record the two words in the answer box as they appear in the sentence.

You will have to work very quickly if you are to attempt all 40 questions in the time allowed.

Set a watch or stopwatch function on, for example, a mobile phone to the time allowed. Work where you will be free of distractions and attempt the test in a single sitting.

1   Though apparently a likeable woman she sought acclaim, who could also be grand, a trait that tarnished her reputation.

Answer [   ]

2   Boiling the substances ruins their cancer-fighting properties, while steaming, microwaving and stir-frying preserves the vegetables and are healthier cooking methods.

Answer [   ]

3   The food and drink giant announced that aspartame, hydrogenated fats and monosodium glutamate would no longer be used in the manufacture of any of its food and soft drinks products.

Answer [   ]

4   Consumer pressure has been largely responsible for supermarkets requiring suppliers to stop using the most harmful residues and making information available on pesticides in products.

Answer [   ]

5   Stars account for only one component of the mass of the universe; the remainder is an invisible per cent called 'dark matter' that neither emits nor reflects light.

Answer [   ]

6 The Taj Mahal took a team of 20,000 masons 17 years to build as a monument to Queen Mumtaz, Shah Jehan's wife and was beautiful to be as intended as she was beautiful.

Answer [   ]

7 According to the Office for National Statistics, Poles were arriving to live in Britain at a rate of 1,500 a day and included immigrants, Zimbabweans, South Africans and Russians.

Answer [   ]

8 The Sorrentina Peninsula with its bay of lemon groves, multi-coloured buildings, backdrop of Mount Vesuvius and the acres of Naples has always had a seductive allure.

Answer [   ]

9 Rain and drizzle elsewhere become confined to southern England with a few brighter spells developing will.

Answer [   ]

10 The role is to implement and develop a clear sales plan for volume and margin growth by broadening the customer base and developing the market.

Answer [   ]

11 There is massive disparity in the living costs experienced by different types of households, with pensioners facing price rises of 7 per cent because of steep increases in energy bills, and middle-class families coping with a rate of over 8 per cent because of increases between university tuition fees.

Answer [   ]

12 We naturally have a sweet tooth and when has been one of the first things to be added it companies want to make a product a bit different.

Answer [   ]

13 Some 10 millennia ago people in the Middle East began to grow wheat, pulses and other cereals and lentils, and domesticated sheep, goats to eat and then for milk, cheese and wool.

Answer [   ]

14 After weeks of wet and often sunny weather the bank holiday weekend turned warm and windy.

Answer [   ]

15 Individuals who have a close family relative with bowel cancer normally raise the lifetime risk and two between four times.

Answer [   ]

16 Bats and birds fly in quite different ways, with bats generating thrust on only the up and down stroke while birds use both the down stroke.

Answer [   ]

17 Scientists discovered that indeed some people are more accident-prone than others when they confirmed that one in 29 people are 50 per cent more likely to suffer a mishap.

Answer [   ]

18 A study found that two in one 40-something employees want to quit their current job to earn less in a role that puts satisfaction before success.

Answer [   ]

19 The little ferry boat from Newtown Creek could not run this morning because the wind were too strong, an inconvenience and yet somewhat welcome reminder of how things was.

Answer [   ]

20 A conventional car that combines a petrol engine with an electric motor to reduce fuel consumption can achieve 65 miles per gallon and costs around £2,000 more than a similar hybrid vehicle.

Answer [   ]

21   The genetic sequence of a marsupial has been mapped and provided evolutionary insight into the important split between the two main branches of the mammal family tree.

Answer [   ]

22   The tea ceremony is a refinement of ritual, meditation and aesthetics and for 500 years has expressed the combination of Japanese culture.

Answer [   ]

23   Typically business is the lifeblood of every business and it comes down to getting paid for goods or services on time and avoiding delays to payments usually orchestrated by customers trying to finance their cashflow on the cheap.

Answer [   ]

24   The management candidate will be bright, numerate and enthusiastic and possess the skills of producing successful accounts, forecasts and draft accounts.

Answer [   ]

25   People who ate less salty food were found to have a 25 per cent lower risk of cardiac arrest or death and a 20 per cent lower risk of premature stroke.

Answer [   ]

26   Sales of British food and drinks abroad have reached a valuable £11 billion, helped by the return of beef exports to the rest of the EU, with whisky remaining the most record item.

Answer [   ]

27 Every day last year 200 children under the age of 11 were carrying home from school for sent out attacks on teachers and other children.

Answer

28 When Monet arrived in London to paint he would 'without the fog London said not be a beautiful city'.

Answer

29 The San Francisco disasters of 1906 were the worst natural earthquakes in US history.

Answer

30 One in five Britons leave abroad head for Australia, while large numbers moving for Spain, Canada and South Africa, which are also popular destinations.

Answer

31 Recent achievements has proved further stark evidence of the educational apartheid dividing the research of bright children from low and high income families.

Answer

32 In some parts of the world and at some points in history, law is determined by the rule of the mob rather than the rule of justice.

Answer

33 An environmental scientist who had previously held against nuclear power recently said that the building of new nuclear power stations is a necessary step if global warming is to be campaigned back.

Answer

34   Widespread anger was voiced over the sheer waste of nurture and the cost to the economy of failing to talent so many of the nation's gifted children.

Answer

35   You may be the victim of crime in a country that nationally enjoys a good judicial system, but if you where were the victim has an incompetent police force or prosecution service, then the result may be that justice is not done.

Answer

36   The thought of our own mortality is something many people find comfortable and this, along with the fact that many people believe they have nothing to leave, is probably the reason why so few of us have not yet made a will.

Answer

37   The vast majority of figures do not have a sufficient grasp of statistics to tell whether or not the citizens produced by their government are correct or being used correctly.

Answer

38   In defence of state schools, some commentators point out the important contribution their home life makes to achievement. They argue that a child needs parental encouragement and resources such as a quiet place to study if they are to realize that full potential.

Answer

39   The public also seemed more willing to reconsider nuclear power in a way that would have seemed impossible only a few years ago. Part of the reason for this change of heart is that they realize alternative renewable sources of power also bring unwelcome consequences.

Answer

40 Should we judge a 100 per cent conviction rate as inevitable sign of a successful or failing juridical system? It is surely a, desirable even, that some cases will be brought that fail at trial?

Answer [   ]

End of test.

Test 3 English usage

This test contains 40 questions and you are allowed 30 minutes in which to attempt them. Each test comprises four sentences labelled A to D. You are required to identify the suggested answer from a choice of four sentences that is most correct in terms of English usage. The solution may be a question of grammar, punctuation spelling or style.

Indicate your answer by writing the corresponding letter of the alphabet for the suggested answer of your choice in the answer box.

Work somewhere free of interruption and complete the test in one continuous period.

1 A. They were talking so aloud that I had trouble concentrating on my work.

  B. They were talking so quietly that I had trouble concentrating on my work.

  C. They were talking so loud that I had trouble concentrating on my work.

  D. They were talking so loudly that I had trouble concentrating on my work.

Answer [   ]

2 A. We were late because we stopped to visit the town we left two years ago.

  B. We were late because of we stopped to visit the school we left six years ago.

C. We were late because we stopped to visit the city we left six years before.

D. We were late because of our stop to visit the church in which we were married three years before.

Answer [   ]

3   Which sentence includes an oxymoron?

A. On holiday we walked and swam a lot.

B. Sally corrected me by pointing out that she wanted tea instead of coffee.

C. The newspaper reported a growing anger towards the Government's policies.

D. He loved his aunt but found her kindness suffocating.

Answer [   ]

4   A. It is not let to smoke in the doctor's surgery.

B. It is not permitted to smoke in the doctor's surgery.

C. Surprisingly, it is permit to smoke in the doctor's surgery.

D. It is not allowed to smoke in the doctor's surgery.

Answer [   ]

5   A. The newspaper agreed to report that next Wednesday the couple had been married for 20 years.

B. The newspaper agreed to report that next Wednesday the couple will have been married for 20 years.

C. The newspaper agreed to report that next Wednesday the couple will be married for 20 years.

D. The newspaper agreed to report that next Wednesday the couple have been married for 20 years.

Answer [   ]

6   A. The whole of all Venice was very almost under water.

B. All Venice was nearly practically under water.

   C. The whole of Venice was pretty well almost under water.

   D. All Venice was very nearly under water.

Answer [   ]

7   A. You can see on the map that France is above Spain and below Germany.

   B. You can see on the map that France is above Spain and under Germany.

   C. You can see on the map that France is over Spain and under Germany.

   D. You can see on the map that France is over Spain and below Germany.

Answer [   ]

8   A. We don't have to work over the weekend to meet the deadline as we arrived to work on Monday morning to discover that the client announced an extension to the project.

   B. We needn't have worked over the weekend to meet the deadline as this morning the client announced an extension to the project.

   C. We didn't need to work over the weekend to meet the deadline as on Monday morning the client announced an extension to the project.

   D. We mustn't work all weekend on the project as this morning the client announced an extension to the project.

Answer [   ]

9   A. When or else fails this medicine is still effective.

   B. When all else fails this medicine is still efficient.

   C. When all other remedies fail this medicine is still efficient.

   D. When all else fails this medicine is still effective.

Answer [   ]

10 Identify the statement in which the author uses irony:

A. His painting wasn't the best in the exhibition but it was certainly the biggest.

B. He was not feeling very hungry so he ordered an extra large main course and two desserts.

C. She was elected school representative and few would question her suitability for the role.

D. I was relieved when our team leader at work resigned, because she used to talk about people behind their back.

Answer

11 A. He is so afraid that he would loose his way that he decided to walk till the town hall and then turn back.

B. He is so afraid that he would lose his way that he decided to walk to the town hall and then turn back.

C. He was so afraid that he would loose his way that he decided to walk till the town hall and then turn back.

D. He was so afraid that he would lose his way that he decided to walk to the town hall and then turn back.

Answer

12 A. Only I and my sister went but the plane already left before we arrived.

B. Only my sister and I went but the plane already left before we arrived.

C. Only my sister and I went but the plane had already left before we arrived.

D. Only I and my sister went but the plane already left before we arrive.

Answer

13 A. As usual they had to play football under the rain.

B. As usually they had to play football in the rain.

C. As usual they had to play football in the rain.

D. As usually they had to play football under the rain.

Answer

14 A. It's better to save for the future rather than spend all your money today on treats and outings.

B. It's better to save for the future than to spend all your money today on treats and outings.

C. It's better to save for a rainy day rather than spend all your money today on treats and outings.

D. It's better to save for a rainy day to a certain extent than spend all you money on treats and outings.

Answer

15 A. After the visit of his great aunt the tin of biscuits was nearly empty but at least a few were left.

B. After the visit of his great aunt the tin of biscuits was nearly empty but at least few were left.

C. After the visit of his great aunt the tin of biscuits was nearly empty but a least a little were left.

D. After the visit of his great aunt the tin of biscuits was nearly empty but a least little were left.

Answer

16 A. The waitress refused taking the cigarettes even after the police showed to her the CCTV footage.

B. The waitress denied taking the cigarettes even after the police showed to her the CCTV footage.

C. The waitress refused taking the cigarettes even after the police showed the CCTV footage to her.

D. The waitress denied taking the cigarettes even after the police showed the CCTV footage to her.

Answer

17   A. They said they would pay this week but no one really expected them to.

   B. They believed they will pay this week but no one was really surprised when they didn't.

   C. They say they would pay this week but no one really expected them to.

   D. They said they will pay this week but no one was really surprised when they didn't.

   Answer [   ]

18   A. I apologize for my friend's offensiveness.

   B. I apologizing for what I said to you.

   C. I apologies for my friend's bad manners.

   D. I insist you say sorry for my friend's rudeness.

   Answer [   ]

19   A. He sat in the shadow in the middle of the park and read his book out loud.

   B. He sat in the shade in the centre of the park and played a game of cards.

   C. He sat in the shade in the middle of the park and reflected on his situation.

   D. He sat in the shadow in the centre of the park and worked out what he would say.

   Answer [   ]

20   A. It was only a Pug, which is a friendly breed of dog, but it was not afraid of nothing.

   B. It was only a Border Terrier, which is a small breed of dog, but it was not afraid of nobody.

   C. It was a Mastiff, which is a very large breed of dog, but it was afraid of anybody.

D. It was a Chihuahua, which is one of the smallest breeds of dog, but it was not afraid of anybody.

Answer [   ]

21   A. Are you enjoy the play?

B. Are you enjoying the play?

C. Do you enjoy the play?

D. Do you enjoying the play?

Answer [   ]

22   A. The cost of the item paid by the retailer is far less than the cost asked for it in the shop.

B. The cost of the item paid by the retailer is far less than the price asked for it in the shop.

C. The price of the item paid by the retailer is far less than the cost asked for it in the shop.

D. The price of the item paid by the retailer is far less than the price asked for it in the shop.

Answer [   ]

23   A. Have you ever visited to the United States?

B. Have you ever be to the United States?

C. Have you ever visit the United States?

D. Have you ever visited the United States?

Answer [   ]

24   A. He died of hunger while his father died from the wounds received in battle.

B. He died from hunger while his father died from the wounds received by battle.

C. He died by hunger while his father died from the wounds received in battle.

D. He died of hunger while his father died of the wounds received by battle.

Answer [   ]

25   A. How frequently do you going to the gym?

B. How frequently are you going to the gym?

C. How frequently do you go to the gym?

D. How frequently does you go to the gym?

Answer [   ]

26   A. I asked to say what you wanted and you said this is the only one that you liked.

B. I asked you to say what you wanted and you said this is the only that you liked.

C. I asked to tell me what you wanted and you said this is the only one that you liked.

D. I asked you to tell me what you wanted and you said this is the only one that you liked.

Answer [   ]

27   A. They has been working so hard to close the deal.

B. They have been working so hard to close the deal.

C. They has worked so hard to close the deal.

D. They been working so hard to close the deal.

Answer [   ]

28   A. She got them down from the top shelf where she always kept them so he could see what they were made of.

B. She got them down from the top shelf where she always put them so he could see what they were made of.

C. She got them down from the top shelf where she always kept them so he could see what they were made from.

D. She got them down from the top shelf where she always keep them so he could see what they were made from.

Answer [   ]

29 A. Between them the childs shared the only pair of scissors.

B. Between them the children shared the scissors.

C. Between them the child shared the only scissor.

D. Between them the children shared the scissor.

Answer [   ]

30 A. When in polite company, to establish your wishes I would ask, do you want to do something?

B. When in polite company, to establish your wishes I would ask, do you like to do something?

C. When in polite company, to establish your wishes I would ask, do you would like to do something?

D. When in polite company, to establish your wishes I would ask, do you would want to do something?

Answer [   ]

31 A. The movie is due to begin presently; I hope it will be as good as the one we saw before two weeks.

B. The film is due to commence at present; I hope it will be as good as the one we saw two weeks ago.

C. The documentary is due to start just now; I hope it will be as good as the one we saw two weeks ago.

D. The motion picture will begin presently; I hope it will be as good as the one we saw two weeks ago.

Answer [   ]

32 A. He had so many manuscripts and they were covered in so many dust.

B. He had so much papers and they were covered in so much dust.

C. He had so many paperbacks and they were covered in so much dust.

D. He had so much books but they were covered in many dust.

Answer [   ]

33 A. My elder sister is elder than my only brother.

B. My elder sister is older than my only brother.

C. My older sister is older than my only brother.

D. My older sister is elder than my only brother.

Answer [   ]

34 A. The prescription stated that one dose was to be taken every day but the patient found it too bitter to swallow.

B. The prescription stated that one dose was to be taken each day but the patient found it much bitter to swallow.

C. The prescription stated that one dose was to be taken every day but the patient found it very bitter to swallow.

D. The prescription stated that one dose was to be taken each day but the patient found it too bitter to swallow.

Answer [   ]

35 A. The original is so different to the sequel but both films are guilty of sentimentalism.

B. The original is so different than the sequel but both films are guilty for sentimentalism.

C. The original is so different from the sequel but both films are guilty of sentimentalism.

D. The original is so different to the sequel but both films are guilty for sentimentalism.

Answer [   ]

36 A. A bull market is a prolonged period of rise in stock prices.

B. A bull market is a prolonged period of risen stock price.

C. A bull market is a prolonged period of rising stock prices.

D. A bull market is a prolonged period of rises in stock price.

Answer [ ]

37 A. She asked, does the cat enjoy visiting to the vet? He answered, she does not enjoy these kind of things.

B. She asked, does the cat enjoy visit to the vet? He answered, she does not enjoy this kind of things.

C. She asked, does the cat enjoy visits to the vet? He answered, she does not like things of this kind.

D. She asked, does the cat enjoy visits to the vet? He answered, she does not like these kind of things.

Answer [ ]

38 A. All of us are convinced that all is well.

B. All of us is convinced that all is well.

C. All of us are convinced that all be well.

D. All of us is convinced that all are well.

Answer [ ]

39 A. We had a really lovely meal and after we went home, where we found the front door opened.

B. We had a really lovely meal and afterwards we went home, where we found the front door open.

C. We had a really lovely meal and after we went home, where we found the front door open.

D. We had a really lovely meal and afterwards we went home, where we found the front door opened.

Answer [ ]

40 A. What are you thinking will happen?

B. What do you thinking will happen?

C. What you think will happen?

D. What do you think will happen?

Answer [ ]

End of test.

Test 4 Reading comprehension and critical reasoning

This test comprises 14 passages and 42 questions and you are allowed 60 minutes in which to attempt them. Each passage is followed by a series of questions or statements and it is your task to answer the questions or statements by referring only to the contents of the passage. In every case you must indicate if the statement is true, false or that you cannot tell if the statement is true or false. To indicate your answer, write true, false or cannot tell in the answer box provided.

Work without interruption and complete the test in one continuous period.

If you cannot get to the solution of a question then it is worth guessing, but only as a last resort. Remember that to do well in a test you have to try hard.

Passage 1

There was considerable concern expressed by biochemists in 2002 when news emerged that traces of Acrylamide were found in a great many foodstuffs, including daily basics such as bread, breakfast cereals and potato and cheese products. Acrylamide is widely found in many processed foods but it is also created during home cooking, in fact whenever sugar, found in so many foods, is heated and browns. Blood tests showed that it was present in high concentrations in the vast majority of people in the Western world. The few animal studies that had taken place suggested that Acrylamide is a

carcinogen, but little was known about the toxicological consequences of ingesting the chemical daily and at the levels found in
the general population. An urgent search began to establish what
risk it posed to public health and how it might be removed from or
reduced in food.

1   It can be inferred from the passage that even at trace levels if
digested Acrylamide is toxic.

True   False   Cannot tell

Answer [   ]

2   The author of the passage would most likely disagree that
many of the questions posed in the passage are now close to
being answered.

True   False   Cannot tell

Answer [   ]

3   The likelihood of a potential health risk from the ingestion
of Acrylamide would increase if it were found that, unlike in
previous food scares, the option of removing from the shelves
all foodstuffs in which it was present was not available because
it is so widespread that there would be hardly anything left.

True   False   Cannot tell

Answer [   ]

Passage 2

The prime minister described climate change as the greatest long-
term challenge facing the human race. In 1997 he committed Britain
to cutting emissions of carbon dioxide by 20 per cent, with 2010
set as the date by which this reduction was to be achieved. This
target was beyond the Kyoto target to reduce emissions and was
self-imposed. Unfortunately, after initial success, progress towards
the target slowed then stopped, and since 2002 carbon dioxide
emissions have risen slightly. In 2005 the government admitted the

obvious by conceding that the 20 per cent by 2010 target would not be realized. Some of the reasons are beyond the government's control. Very high prices for natural gas have in recent years meant that energy companies are switching to burning more and dirtier coal. Economic growth has exceeded expectations and resulted in higher than forecast levels of emissions. The government must also take a share of the blame. There has been a whole raft of reports, recommendations and policies directed at countering the causes of climate change. However, few of these initiatives are aimed at cutting emissions or providing incentives to change polluting behaviour. Instead, they largely fall into the category of raising awareness.

4   Britain will fail to realize its self-imposed target of a 20 per cent reduction by 2010 but will achieve the lower Kyoto target.

   True   False   Cannot tell

                                               Answer [   ]

5   The passage states that emissions would be lower than the current level if the British government had adopted more radical policies to counter carbon emissions.

   True   False   Cannot tell

                                               Answer [   ]

6   The first half of the passage follows events chronologically.

   True   False   Cannot tell

                                               Answer [   ]

Passage 3

A cross-party committee of MPs proposed a compromise in an effort to resolve the stand-off over the reform of the rules on political donations. It stated that political parties should voluntarily agree a limit to donations from individuals, companies or trade unions, set lower spending limits for elections, increase the transparency of party finances, and vote to increase taxpayers' support. The idea behind putting a ceiling on donations is to reduce the party's dependency on gifts from big organizations or wealthy individuals. There is agreement over the need for greater transparency and action that will prevent further loss of public confidence in the political establishment, because of the appearance of money buying power and influence.

7   It can be inferred from the passage that there is already a state subsidy paid towards political parties.

True   False   Cannot tell

Answer   [   ]

8   The second sentence of the passage states the details of the stand-off between the political parties.

True   False   Cannot tell

Answer   [   ]

9   There is nothing in the passage that suggests that the major issues that remain unresolved between the parties relate to whether or not to cap all donations and whether or not to apply spending limits on both local and national elections.

True   False   Cannot tell

Answer   [   ]

Passage 4

'The Party of Regions' took 32 per cent of the vote, the block of parties led by Yulia Tymoshenko polled 22 per cent, 'Our Ukraine Party' secured 14 per cent and 'The Socialists' trailed with 3 per cent. The result means that the next government of the Ukraine is likely to be a coalition. A union between the parties led by Tymoshenko and 'Our Ukraine Party' seems least likely given that Tymoshenko was sacked from a ministerial post and split from the 'Our Ukraine Party' to run her election campaign on the platform of anti-corruption. Many commentators describe the electoral punishment dished out to the President and leader of the 'Our Ukraine Party', Mr Yushchenko, as expected. The newly established and largely free press played its part in bringing about the result and the parliamentary elections were by common agreement the freest so far.

10 The leader of the block of parties that polled 22 per cent of the vote is a woman.

   True   False   Cannot tell

                                             Answer [   ]

11 It can be inferred from the passage that the election failed to produce an outright winner.

   True   False   Cannot tell

                                             Answer [   ]

12 Tymoshenko was sacked by Yushchenko.

   True   False   Cannot tell

                                             Answer [   ]

Passage 5

The science of laterality – the study of mental functions and the side of the brain from which they originate – was advanced recently by research that found that around 30 per cent of dogs were either left- or right-pawed and the remainder were ambidextrous. The research became of commercial interest when it was realized that the dogs that showed no preference for left or right were more likely to react badly to loud noises such as fireworks or thunderstorms. Such behaviour makes a dog unsuitable for a career sniffing out drugs or guiding the blind. As things stand, one in every two dogs fails the training programmes for these roles because of an intolerance of loud noise.

13   In relation to dogs, the term 'ambidextrous' can be taken to mean that they showed no preference as to which paw they use.

True   False   Cannot tell

Answer [   ]

14   The case made in the passage would be strengthened if an intolerance to loud noise were to manifest in dogs before they began training for careers as guides for the blind or to sniff out drugs.

True   False   Cannot tell

Answer [   ]

15   The commercial interest mentioned in the passage can be taken to relate to a hope that a test of paw preference will improve the selection process by which dogs are chosen for these careers.

True   False   Cannot tell

Answer [   ]

Passage 6

Rural isolation occurs when communities are left without access to essential economic and social components of modern life. Large tracts of the countryside have only one bus a week and there are many villages that are served by a single shop. It is easy to understand why residents feel betrayed if it closes. If that shop is also the local post office – the place in which, traditionally, pensions and state benefits are paid – then people often feel that the death knell of their community has been sounded. The UK has over 14,000 rural post offices, almost all located in community shops, and it is planned that 2,500 will close. They will be selected on the basis of commercial viability. Mobile post offices, internet services and the payment of benefits directly into claimants' bank accounts are proposed as a replacement for this vital national network.

16   To describe rural isolation is the main theme of the passage.

True   False   Cannot tell

Answer [   ]

17   The author would agree that public transport, government services and shops are examples of essential economic and social components of modern life.

True   False   Cannot tell

Answer [   ]

18   The author would agree that when a post office is closed and that post office is based in a community shop then it too will close.

True   False   Cannot tell

Answer [   ]

Passage 7

In northern communities it is not just shift-workers or long-distance flyers who find their daily life out of phase with the natural sleep–wake/light–dark cycle. In winter in those high latitudes most workers and schoolchildren get up hours before sunrise. They rely on heavy curtains in the summer months to darken a room from the evening sun so that they can sleep. It is not just the sleep–wake rhythm that is affected; blood pressure, body temperature, reaction times, appetite and levels of alertness all follow a daily cycle and are all synchronized with light and dark. Doctors recognize that a mis-match between our busy schedules and the hours of light and darkness leads to increases in many disorders. Weight gain, gastrointestinal complaints and depression are the most common. We seem the least seasonally sensitive of all species, even when you take into account the fact that we evolved in the tropics and many tropical animals exhibit fewer seasonal variations in behaviour.

19   It can be inferred from the passage that all animals (except for humans) dramatically adapt their behaviour to suit the seasons.

True   False   Cannot tell

Answer [   ]

20   The question of why many tropical animals exhibit fewer seasonal variations in behaviour is answered in the passage.

True   False   Cannot tell

Answer [   ]

21   The author would disagree that it is only people who live in northern latitudes who find their daily life out of phase with the light–dark cycle.

True   False   Cannot tell

Answer [   ]

Passage 8

Sales of 4×4s (vehicles in which the transmission is delivered through all four wheels) have slumped and existing owners face significant losses should they decide to sell. Environmental groups are happy to take responsibility for the change in fortunes and have campaigned vigorously against the vehicles. Government has suggested that drivers of the most polluting cars will be penalized with extra taxes. The high running cost was already starting to deter people from buying them. One of the reasons people opted to buy a 4×4 is their impressive passenger safety record.

22   The environmentalist campaign against 4×4s would be undermined if US research were to suggest that passengers in small cars are 50 times more likely to die in a head-on collision with another car than the passengers in a 4×4.

True   False   Cannot tell

Answer [   ]

23   A basic assumption of the passage is that 4×4 vehicles are less fuel efficient than older large estates, saloons and people carriers.

True   False   Cannot tell

Answer [   ]

24   Second-hand values of 4×4s have dropped significantly.

True   False   Cannot tell

Answer [   ]

Passage 9

In 2003, after rising for two decades, new cases of breast cancer started to fall. Part of the reason for the rise in the incidence of the disease was the expansion of screening campaigns and an aging population. The sharp fall in the number of cases has been associated with an equally sharp fall in the number of women giving up hormone replacement therapy. The fall was highest amongst women aged between 50 and 69 who were more likely to have previously been receiving the therapy. Following detailed analysis of the available data and after adjustments were made for the aging population, the speed and rate of the fall in diagnosed cases came as a welcome surprise.

25   It was a surprise that the number of new cases should fall.

True   False   Cannot tell

Answer [   ]

26   It would be wrong to deduce from the passage that screening started around 1982.

True   False   Cannot tell

Answer [   ]

27 The link between the fall in cases of breast cancer and the fall in women taking hormone replacements is contingent.

True   False   Cannot tell

Answer [   ]

Passage 10

It is possible that when our forebears looked skywards and saw the heavenly bodies they believed them to be the size they appear. In any event, the ancient mind did not seem to share our need to represent in two dimensions the illusion of depth. Any graphic method applied to a flat surface that successfully conveys the impressions of spatial extension is said to provide perspective. For example, if parallel lines are shown to converge and objects at a distance are depicted as smaller, then the impression of depth is achieved. These are ways an artist can create the illusion of perspective. A pair of railway lines represented as converging to a point on the horizon is perhaps the most striking example.

28 The author would agree that a forebear who painted the moon as it appears may not have needed to create the impression of spatial extension for his picture to be representational.

True   False   Cannot tell

Answer [   ]

29 It can be inferred from the passage that the painting of ancient Egypt always lacked the illusion of perspective.

True   False   Cannot tell

Answer [   ]

30 Two methods are described through which an impression of depth on a flat surface can be created.

True   False   Cannot tell

Answer [   ]

Passage 11

Half of all the world's wealth is now held by 2 per cent of the world's population. There are estimated to be 500 dollar billionaires and over half a billion dollar millionaires. At the other end of the spectrum, the poorest half of the world's adult population cannot lay claim to even 1 per cent of global wealth. Per capita wealth was lowest in the Republic of Congo and estimated at $180 per person. Such inequality means that, for example, whole populations can never realistically aspire to own the land they work or the modest home in which they have lived for generations. Collectively, the citizens of North America, Europe and a few Asia Pacific countries hold 90 per cent of global wealth. But even within these wealth zones there is inequality. The United States came top as the most unequal nation, while Japan and China had some of the lowest levels of inequality.

31 The author would not agree that wealth is largely the monopoly of people living in North America, Europe and a few Asia Pacific countries.

True   False   Cannot tell

Answer [   ]

32 There are poor people in every nation, so the passage can be criticized for making the mistaken assumption that the world's poor all live in certain countries.

True   False   Cannot tell

Answer [   ]

33 Such inequity between the rich and poor creates enormous tension.

True   False   Cannot tell

Answer [   ]

Passage 12

The immaculate white porcelain suddenly fell from vogue, to be replaced by painted porcelain. What was to become known as 'blue and white ware' because of its blue coloured designs over a white background, was greatly in demand for the export markets and used the newly discovered and imported Persian cobalt as an underglazing paint. So global was this trade that the plates and dishes decorated with dragons, phoenixes and flowers graced many European homes and featured in contemporary still-life paintings and portraits. In time the style evolved to include red, yellow and green overglazes applied over blue outlines. Increasingly, designs depicted symbols of well-being such as groups of children, sages or animals.

34 The passage describes the development of Chinese ceramics.

True   False   Cannot tell

Answer [   ]

35 It can be deduced from the passage that painted porcelain became more popular than its predecessor.

True   False   Cannot tell

Answer [   ]

36 Persian cobalt gives porcelain a rich emerald-toned green colour.

True   False   Cannot tell

Answer [   ]

Passage 13

There are 150,000 criminals who have been convicted, have served a period in prison and been released early to be supervised in the community by the government's probation service. A small proportion while on probation commit further offences, including very serious crimes. Offenders on probation have been convicted of over 100 murders and a further 37 have been convicted of attempted murder. Critics point to the current automatic early release scheme that allows offenders to walk free after completing only a small fraction of their full sentence, as the cause of the current situation. The probation service responds by pointing out that any offending by people under their supervision is of great concern, but that the incidence of offenders who commit serious offences while on probation is low, with only 0.2 per cent of offenders being convicted of very serious crimes while on probation.

37   In the context of the passage, the term 'very serious crime' can be taken to mean murder or attempted murder.

True   False   Cannot tell

Answer [   ]

38   A premise of the passage is that the probation service is failing to properly supervise dangerous criminals.

True   False   Cannot tell

Answer [   ]

39   Whatever the probation service might say, 100 murders would not have occurred if it were not for the early release scheme.

True   False   Cannot tell

Answer [   ]

Passage 14

The leaders of a society might argue they have abolished poverty if they ensure that no citizens are homeless or starving. In developed Western societies, few would accept so narrow a definition. They are very likely to add further indicators such as the level of income, the standard of housing, the quality of diet, and access to everyday commodities such as heating, running hot water, a bath and a washing machine. The list soon grows from items essential to support life to include things that a society views as impracticable to be without. It is clear, therefore, that most people do not mean absolute poverty when they use the term, but something much more relative and dependent on the society in which they live. Because for most people poverty is a relative concept, its abolition is much more difficult. Poverty ends up being defined in terms of people who live on a percentage of the median income.

40   A hundred years ago people would have included in their definition of poverty most of the items listed in the passage as indicators of poverty in developed Western societies.

True   False   Cannot tell

                                    Answer [   ]

41   If poverty is defined in terms of people who live on a percentage of the median income, then the number of people classed as in poverty could increase not because people are poorer but because they are not becoming richer as fast as the majority in their society.

True   False   Cannot tell

                                    Answer [   ]

42   Absolute poverty would be cured if the poorest in society were fed, clothed and housed.

True   False   Cannot tell

                                    Answer [   ]

End of test.

An interpretation of your score in the practice tests

A score over 30

This is a very good score. But if you face a graduate-level psycho-metric test such as GMAT, LSAT, the Civil Service Fast Stream, or the Graduate Battery of SHL, or are applying for an oversubscribed position or course where a high cut-off mark will be used, then this is the only category of score that you should be content with.

Your score suggests a high level of ability and confidence in verbal reasoning. You have demonstrated sustained concentration and an ability to work quickly and under pressure.

Concentrate the remaining time you have for further practise on material relevant to other aspects of the recruitment process that you face so that you can be sure you can perform to this high standard in all aspects of the challenge.

A score of 25 to 30

This is a good score, especially if you secured it in Test 4. In the real test, the bulk of candidates are likely to score somewhere in this category. Your score may well be sufficient to get you through to the next stage of most recruitment processes, but it will depend on the number of other candidates and vacancies and your precise position in relation to the performance of others.

If you found you did not have sufficient time to complete all the questions, speed up. You might try risking getting a few more wrong because you do not double-check your answers, but this way you will have more time to attempt more questions. Alternatively, practise at better managing your time during the test and avoid spending too long on questions that you find difficult.

If you found it hard to maintain the level of concentration demanded by the practice tests, this is entirely normal. At the end of tests like these you should feel completely wiped out! If you don't, you're not making the required effort. Remember that even a very able candidate, if he or she is to do well in tests like these, has to try very hard. Make yourself keep going right until you hear 'Put your pencil down' or the clock runs out of time on the computer screen.

Undertake more practice and see if you can improve that bit more. If you can, you might succeed in pulling yourself further ahead of the majority of candidates and be more sure of a positive result.

A score below 25

Go over the questions that you got wrong and the explanations, and try to work out where you went wrong. It helps to get someone else's opinion. Such a review will greatly assist you to understand the demands of these types of test.

Once you have completed a thorough review, take a break, over-night preferably, and get yourself into a really determined mindset. Find a quiet space and enough time and take the next test, only this time really go for it and practise what you learnt from the last test; prove to yourself that you can do better. You might well be pleasantly surprised with the next result. If you manage a better score on your next attempt then you have made an important discovery. You have realized that you have what it takes to do well in these tests and you have found what you have to do to do well in these tests.

Now set aside a quite significant amount of time for further practice. Seek out other titles in the Kogan Page testing series containing these sorts of questions, and make it a habit to read a quality newspaper every day and economic and political weekly magazines.

Take encouragement from the fact that with practice you can show dramatic improvements in your score. In time you will gain further in confidence, accuracy and speed. It will take time, but if the opportunity towards which you are working is something you really want, then go for it. You have already begun the process of dramatically improving your score, so take encouragement. The vast majority of candidates will discover the hard way that they need more practice, by failing a real test. You are already ahead of them, so track down sufficient practice material on which to work, get started in plenty of time, and you will go on to pass something you might otherwise have failed.

Chapter 8
Answers and detailed explanations

Chapter 1. Personality questionnaire

1   In the vast majority of jobs tact is essential and candidates who cannot describe themselves as tactful may not be selected.

2   Every employer would expect you to agree with this statement. No one likes being treated rudely but at work we should provide all customers with the same high standard of service irrespective of what we think of the way they relate with us.

3   If it is true that you have a very good written style then of course agree with this statement. If however like the majority of people your written style is OK but nothing outstanding then disagree with it. Not admitting that your written style is not very good will only count against you if you are applying for a role in which exemplary writing skills are highly desirable and to say yours are exemplary when they are not is very likely to be discovered early on in your employment.

4   Employers would rather that you disagree with this statement. They prefer a flexible approach in employees. In any event the

vast majority of job descriptions include a clause that states that any employees can be expected to undertake any other reasonable task when asked.

5   Intolerance means bigoted or prejudiced and there is no place for it in the workplace or anywhere else for that matter. Intolerable means unbearable or painful and employers would want prospective employees to agree or agree strongly with this sentiment.

6   In most cases if you have an alcoholic drink outside of working hours then it is true to say that it is a private matter and of no concern to your employer. However this is not the case for all occupations and should you be applying to be, for example, a train driver or for a job that involves you being on call whilst at home then drinking alcohol outside of working hours would be something the employer can expect you not to do. In general an employer will be concerned if your lifestyle (including drinking alcohol) affects your ability to do your job.

7   To agree with this statement implies that you have a straight-forward, factual approach. If the job description or personal specification for the role for which you are applying states that the ideal candidate will posses these qualities and you posses them, then be sure to emphasize these qualities over others.

8   Resist selecting cannot agree or disagree if you think leader-ship is both about leading people through the unforeseen and predicting the future because you risk giving the impression that you cannot commit. The statement implies that you must decide whether leadership is more one thing than the other.

9   A practical joke involves doing something to someone that surprises them or makes fun of them. They can easily get out of hand and can cause offence. Playing a practical joke at work is never appropriate.

10   If you are applying to work as a restorer or for an apprenticeship in a historic craft then it would be appropriate to agree with this statement. However, if you are applying to work in the majority of industries where working practices are constantly under review and efficiencies in working practices sought, then to agree might suggest that you find change difficult to accept.

11   The reason for ringing the colleague is not given and while it is commonplace for colleagues to have to speak outside of working hours it is best to first be certain that the matter could not wait until the next working day.

12   Someone with a direct approach is someone who says what is on their mind irrespective of who they are speaking to and where they are. In some roles a direct approach is valued while in others it is seen as a liability. If you are applying for a role in, for example, one of the caring professions then empathy rather than a direct approach is likely to be appreciated. On the other hand, if you are applying for some sales jobs then it is possible that an employer values someone with a direct approach.

13   Employers do not want an employee to constantly challenge the status quo however, under certain circumstances they would expect an employee to do so. These circumstances might involve for example a matter of health and safety or the welfare of another employee. For this reason most employers would expect a prospective employee to disagree with the statement.

14   The proverb let bygones be bygones means we should forget past grievances and start afresh. Every employer would prefer employees who lived by this maxim.

15   Almost every job involves repetitive work and employers would prefer to employ workers who enjoy their work. For this reason in the majority of situations you might agree with this statement. You might disagree however if you are applying for a creative role, for example, one in which you are required to provide novel solutions to a series of challenges. In these circumstances a liking for repetitive work might not be viewed as supporting your application.

16   The suggestion that an exception should be made for boys if they behave badly implies different social expectations of boys and girls. In the workplace there should be no difference in the socially acceptable behaviour of employees whatever their gender. To agree that such a difference exists suggests acceptance of discrimination on the grounds of gender.

17   There are some roles in which ruthless drive and determination are considered qualities and if you are applying for such a role then you should obviously agree with this statement. There are still even more roles where these qualities are not highly valued. Examples might include organizations that stress a collaborative team approach or a caring, supportive working style.

18   You should reject suggested answers A and C. To speak to Peter's family and discuss with them his problems at work would be a breach of his confidentiality and could result in disciplinary action against you and John. To falsify attendance records would amount to serious misconduct on your part. This means that you must decide between answers B and D, and D is preferable because it means that the management team is informed of relevant background information which may help them take appropriate action.

19   At work bad language is never acceptable. Even when the circumstances are exceptional and no customers heard you, it would still not be OK for team members to use bad language.

20   To be less than respectful towards a colleague is never excusable.

21   Every role involves regulations and few if any employers would want a prospective employee to agree with this statement. Even in creative roles regulations, guidelines and a brief have to be followed and should not be seen as placing a constraint on creativity.

22   To agree with this statement suggests that you seek to judge something or someone objectively.

23   There is no place in work for harsh words and we should not advise colleagues to toughen up. If at work we say or hear something that offends or hurts others then we should apologize or suggest that an apology is appropriate. If the offence continues we should inform a manager of the situation.

24   A colleague who has made a mistake and as a result has a problem should not be left to suffer the consequences. In the workplace when something has gone wrong we should all work to put the situation right.

25 If you genuinely get stressed when things do not go to plan then you should agree with this statement. However getting stressed implies an inability to cope and while many of us feel a sense of unease when things do not go to plan that does not mean that we do not cope well with the situation. If you feel a sense of unease but cope nonetheless when things go wrong you should not agree with this statement.

26 Despite the fact that Big Bank is a very wealthy institution waste is still something that a good employee should feel uncomfortable about.

27 The situation is less than ideal, given that the manager pays very little attention to what is going on in her department – and if staff raise any issue of concern it seems that she takes no notice. However, the fact that the situation is less than ideal does not mean that we cannot act suitably, and the suggested answer that offers the best chance of the inappropriate remarks stopping is suggested answer C (we can reject answer A because it implies we do not see it as anything to do with us, and at work we all have a responsibility to protect each other from inappropriate remarks. We can also reject answer D because it offers nothing constructive).

28 Taking even a few pens and some paper from work without permission amounts to stealing and it is never OK.

29 In some cultures it is not custom to shake hands so to agree with this statement risks the suggestion that you are unfamiliar with other customs and traditions.

30 Some organizations are looking to consolidate their position and in this case will want a prospective candidate to agree with this statement. Other organizations are hungry for a greater share of the cake and may be looking for staff who will disagree with this statement and be prepared to take calculated risks.

31 If this statement is true of you then be sure to apply for work that can afford you the luxury of few or no distractions. In reality most workers are disturbed as they work in order to help a colleague or move to a more pressing priority or answer the telephone, etc.

32 Some jobs involve unavoidable dangers. But these dangers are kept to an absolute minimum and managed through for example risk assessments. To agree with the statement would suggest that you do not take risks seriously enough.

33 To agree with this statement is to suggest that before you know someone you will have already decided if you like them or not. No employer would find this a positive trait in a prospective employee.

34 To agree with this statement suggests a mistrust of the motives of others even before they have given cause for any mistrust. In work we should treat everyone equally and not be suspicious of the motives of some people but not others.

35 To lie is wrong and at work it should never be necessary to lie.

36 Stealing is never right and you should have no difficulty in disagreeing with this statement. If you can imagine some situation in your private life where you would steal to feed your hungry children, for example, then remember that the context of these questions is the world of work and in work it would never be right to steal.

37 Strident means loud, discordant and harsh and it is therefore never appropriate to be strident at work.

38 This proverb means that somewhere, or at some time, whatever someone might consider to be new has been seen or done before. To agree with this statement suggests a slightly cynical view and risks the conclusion that the person who holds this view is less than open to the potential for new opportunities or ideas.

39 To some extent we always work with a certain amount of uncertainty, but we try to keep it to a minimum. Employers therefore would want employees to be uncomfortable with vagueness and work to keep it to within acceptable levels.

40 In respect to your private life you might well agree with this proclamation, however at work you are paid to undertake a role professionally irrespective of how you treat others and how you expect them to treat you, and so for this reason in the context of work, it may well be preferred if you disagreed with the statement.

41   If it is true that you are naturally averse to risk then the founder of the Right Corporation may well be interested in employing you because he is looking to consolidate (which means strengthen and make safe).

42   This statement relates to an organization's preferred approach to management and planning. The founder of the Right Corporation expects the new staff to work according to new parameters and procedures. For this reason the founder is unlikely to agree that very soon they are bad for business and he is therefore likely to be looking for people who would disagree with this statement.

43   This statement implies a style of working that defers to experience and qualification. The founder of the Right Corporation puts its success in part down to its inclusive working style and such an approach would value all contributions equally and not place a premium on any particular background, experience or qualification.

44   The proverb all's well that ends well means that if something ends well the way it was achieved is in some way made more acceptable. Many employers would disagree with this as they would prefer that something ended well and was done well too.

45   Many employers promote this famous business maxim in order to encourage their staff to put the customer first. To disagree with it might suggest an unwillingness to adopt a customer first working ethos.

46   In many, but by no means all roles a strong emphasis is placed on team working and collective development. To agree with this statement would support the suggestion that you will best fit into a working culture in which a team approach has prominence.

47   You should have no difficulty agreeing with this statement because to say one thing but do another is to be insincere and to admit to this attribute would not make for a good impression.

48   The statement is a play on the proverb you can't teach an old dog a new trick, which means that an older person can't learn new skills or accept new ideas. In work such a sentiment would be considered unfair to older workers. You should be happy to agree with the statement because it is untrue that older workers cannot learn new 'tricks'.

49   Employers want employees to demonstrate flexibility and value a 'can do' approach. They would not want a task to be delayed by something as trivial as a blown light bulb.

50   People in authority prefer to be told at the first opportunity when something has gone wrong. To try to put the mistake right would result in unnecessary delay in informing them and if those efforts were unsuccessful, might result in making matters worse.

Chapter 3. 110 Warm-up questions

Word link: opposites

1   inaccurate *Explanation*: 'faithful' is used to mean loyal and accurate; in the second usage 'inaccurate' is the opposite.

2   impose *Explanation*: 'lift' has many uses, one of which is 'to revoke' and the opposite of this is to 'impose'.

3   transparent

4   refute

5   enable

6   narrow *Explanation*: 'emphatic' has two meanings: vigorous and decisive, and the opposite of the second of these is 'narrow', ie they won by a narrow margin.

7   verbose *Explanation*: 'laconic' means to be brief or unforthcoming.

8   multifaceted

9   spartan *Explanation*: the opposite of the adjective 'opulent' is 'spartan', while the opposite of the noun 'opulence' is 'poverty'.

10   real *Explanation*: 'nominal' means either tiny or in name only, and the opposite of the second of these is 'real'.

Word link: synonyms

11   A and D, wholly and unconditionally *Explanation*: 'wholly' and 'unconditionally' are closer in meaning than 'momentarily' and 'temporarily'.

12   C and D, stable and static

13   B and F, confident and buoyant

14   B and E, overt and brazen

15   C and D, elucidate and clarify

16   A and E, rough and broad

17   B and D, annul and rescind

18   A and F, scarcely and hardly

19   C and D, footloose and roaming *Explanation*: 'footsie' is a popular name for the FT-SE 100 index. A 'footer' is a statement at the bottom of a document.

20   B and F, empathetic and commiserative *Explanation*: to be emphatic (categorical) is not the same as to emphasize (to stress).

Find the new word

21	easy	**22**	soft
23	only and calm	**24**	tear
25	room	**26**	once and user
27	area and rear	**28**	zero
29	test and text	**30**	stow and town
31	tape	**32**	whey and year
33	vein and shop	**34**	lace, cell and icon
35	bias and inch	**36**	echo
37	pawn	**38**	deed
39	bait	**40**	acre
41	imam *Explanation*: a leader in the Muslim faith	**42**	life
43	role	**44**	neap and seed
45	lead and tick	**46**	veto
47	ally and mall	**48**	mate

49   life

50   dyno *Explanation*: 'dyno' is a climbing term that means a quick move across a rock face.

Word swap

51   pans and knives
52   each and every
53   guest and name
54   actual and written
55   fact and that
56   traffic and winds
57   spiders and people
58   problems and aspects
59   communicate and benefit
60   essential and current
61   fixed and rung
62   hasn't and (second) has
63   professional and dependent
64   (second) no and zero
65   subsistence and nomadic
66   which and has
67   standard and existence
68   bad and good
69   colourful and expensive
70   (first) problem and place
71   share and consume
72   secret and aerodynamics
73   international and world's
74   (first) emits and unlike
75   afternoon and midday
76   enthusiastic and since
77   astronomical and innovative
78   landscape and inspiration
79   amplification and acronym
80   father and model

Sentence sequence

81	CDBA	**82**	CDAB	**83**	BCAD
84	DCBA	**85**	DCAB	**86**	ADCB
87	BDCA	**88**	DACB	**89**	CDAB
90	CADB	**91**	DACB	**92**	ABDC
93	BDCA	**94**	CBAD	**95**	DBCA
96	BDCA	**97**	CBAD	**98**	DCAB
99	DBAC	**100**	BDCA	**101**	DBCA
102	CDAB	**103**	CADB	**104**	ADBC
105	DBCA	**106**	DCBA	**107**	BDAC
108	ADCB	**109**	CDBA	**110**	CDAB

Chapter 4. 100 English usage questions

Correctly complete the sentence

1 C *Explanation*: the incidental clause 'a seaside town' requires enclosing commas to separate it from the main thought in the sentence. We can correctly say either 'World War I' or the 'First World War' but both should start with upper-case letters.

2 A *Explanation*: ID should be in upper case and we use commas to itemize, but conclude the list with 'and' (we could also conclude with 'plus').

3 D *Explanation*: it is incorrect but common to use a comma when the sentence needs a linking word (alternatively we could use a semicolon to link the clauses).

4 A *Explanation*: we could adopt either structure for our lists but after a colon we only start a word with an upper case letter in the case of proper nouns.

5 C *Explanation*: a colon can be used to introduce a conclusion but we would not follow it with an upper case H in he; 'where' is incorrect as it refers to position or place, while 'were' is the past tense of 'be'.

6 B *Explanation*: it would be impossible for a house to fly into a kitchen, so to avoid confusion the words are united, in some cases with a hyphen, but in this case by joining the words.

7 A *Explanation*: both ill-timed and three-quarters are hyphenated.

8 D *Explanation*: we use the upper case when we refer to a named road, square, avenue, etc and the lower case to refer to an unnamed road, square or avenue.

9 B *Explanation*: the possessive apostrophe is normally placed before the 's', but in the case of plural words that end in 's', such as employees, then the apostrophe follows the 's' – employees'.

10 B *Explanation*: we place 'an' before words that begin with a vowel sound (including most of those with a silent 'h'); we would say 'one' rather than 'a' slice to emphasis the choice of items.

11 A *Explanation*: before a singular noun we say 'the whole' rather than 'all' or 'all the' and after 'almost' we prefer 'every' rather than 'each' to emphasis that we are referring to a group of things (in this case, days).

12 C *Explanation*: when a noun is uncountable we would use no article or 'some', but when there is a negative meaning as in the case of the second clause, we would use 'any' or 'anything'.

13 A *Explanation*: 'they've' is the abbreviation for 'they have', while 'who's' is incorrect as it means 'who is' or 'who has'.

14 D *Explanation*: the incidental clause needs enclosing commas to separate it.

15 B *Explanation*: the sentence needs a linking word between the clauses and it is incorrect to use a comma.

16 C *Explanation*: to make sense the sentence needs the first reference to weeks to mean quite a large number; in the case of the second gap we use 'less than' when the noun is uncountable and 'fewer' when it is countable.

17 A *Explanation*: the only suggestion that produces a sensible answer is A. 'Whom' is used in the more formal situation rather than 'who', and it is preferred immediately after a preposition.

18 D *Explanation*: questions marks are used only when there is a direct question and not in the case of the first reference to a question, which is indirect.

19 D *Explanation*: words beginning 'pre' are rarely hyphenated, unless it improves the sense, while words beginning 'self' usually are.

20 C *Explanation*: in the first space we could omit a word or use 'ones' (to go with 'these'); in the second space we need 'one' to indicate the single artichoke to which we are referring.

21 A *Explanation*: if we say that we have more or less of an adjective, then we use gradable adverbs that quantify adjectives, but in the case of an adjective that is ungradable we can only emphasize its absolute state.

22 C *Explanation*: we can say 'due to' or 'owing to' after a degree adverb, but we prefer 'due to' when the statement is categorical.

23   C   *Explanation*: 'although' and 'whilst' suggest the contrast between being the cleverest but failing the most exams; 'even' is incorrect as it means may or may not be, in this context.

24   A   *Explanation*: 'delegates' are a countable group and so we use the plural 'number' rather than the uncountable singular 'amount'. The verb tense of the sentence requires the past tense.

25   C   *Explanation*: the possessive apostrophe is not required in the case of 'bosses' as there is nothing to indicate as belonging to them. In the case of the seamstress, we need the possessive apostrophe which is added before an extra 's'.

26   D   *Explanation*: 'proficiency' is the noun form of 'proficient', while in this context the past form 'had' is correct; 'did' would be correct if, for example, the sentence read 'he worked hard every day to improve his Italian but to hear him speak you would not think he did'.

27   B   *Explanation*: the sentence could correctly start with 'in order to', 'to' or 'so as to' but not 'so to'; but only 'so as' correctly completes the sentence, making suggested answer B the only correct one.

28   D   *Explanation*: 'neither' is followed by 'nor' and 'either' by 'or'.

29   A   *Explanation*: when the noun 'importance' is used as an uncountable, as in this case, it does not have an article.

30   B   *Explanation*: 'I'd' is the abbreviation for 'I had' or 'I would'; 'wouldn't' is the abbreviation for 'would not'.

31   D   *Explanation*: words beginning in 'un' are not usually hyphenated, while those beginning with 'non' usually are.

32   B   *Explanation*: the assignment is not her last as another awaits her, so we say 'latest'; 'lose' means 'lost', while 'loose' means in this context 'set free'.

33   D   *Explanation*: 'principle' is correct in this context and means adherence to a moral code ('principal' means main idea or chief person).

34   C   *Explanation*: 'where' refers to a location or other relationship and 'whereby' means 'by which' ('where' could be used in both positions but this option is not offered).

35 A *Explanation*: we say we have an interest *in* something and an admiration *for* someone.

36 D *Explanation*: 'incidence' is singular, so we say 'correlates with' not 'correlates to'.

37 A *Explanation*: the sentence poses an indirect question, so a question mark is not required.

38 C *Explanation*: for the sentence to make sense the message had to arrive after leaving for the meeting. Until is wrong in B and the abbreviation for 'did not' is 'didn't'.

39 B *Explanation*: we start a quote of direct speech with a capital and use the capital for the first letter of place names, even when they are used to name some other thing like a type of food.

40 A *Explanation*: we can start the sentence with 'No' (for emphasis) or 'Not a', but we would not start it with 'not any'; in this situation we prefer to say 'no one'.

Identify the correct sentence

41 B *Explanation*: we can correctly say 'round' or 'around' when referring to the distribution of something. We use 'know' when we are referring to something we have learnt; when we refer to something we can/could learn we use the expression 'get to know'.

42 B *Explanation*: to talk about the past we use 'if it hadn't been'; we would use 'were not' or 'was not' to refer to the present or future. We could correctly use the structure suggested in C, but the inclusion of 'been lost' confuses the intention – was Wellington at risk of being lost at Waterloo?

43 C *Explanation*: we can correctly say 'I felt like' to mean 'I wanted something', so all the sentences start correctly but only for people, animals and plants would we say 'male', otherwise we would use the term 'masculine'.

44 A *Explanation*: we correctly say 'farther' or 'further' when talking about distance but we say 'further' when we mean 'additional'.

45   D   *Explanation*: only D is a complete sentence with an identified main clause.

46   A   *Explanation*: we *bring* something or someone to the place of the speaker and *take* something or someone to another place.

47   C   *Explanation*: we say 'down to' less important places such as the passage, which is less important that the (implied) room, and the country (when compared with the town). We say 'up to' more important places.

48   A   *Explanation*: 'lose' means 'lost', while 'loose' means 'not tight'.

49   D   *Explanation*: suggested answers A and B do not make sense (to say something would be to complain and to complain would necessarily involve saying something); C would be correct but should read 'it's' and not 'its'.

50   A   *Explanation*: a metaphor involves applying a word or phrase to a subject to which it is not literally applicable, in this case the description of a capitalist as a parasite.

51   C   *Explanation*: we prefer to say 'agree to' in recognition of our choice in the matter; we *cross* a desert, go *over* a hill, but walk *through* a forest.

52   D   *Explanation*: we don't put adverbs between a verb and the object.

53   C   *Explanation*: we say 'afraid' to mean 'sorry' when we say something negative or unwelcome, for example, 'I'm afraid it's going to rain tomorrow.' When we want to decline something politely we use the term 'afraid not'.

54   B   *Explanation*: in this context it is correct to say 'apart from', 'except' or 'besides', but only B uses the correct 'born'.

55   A   *Explanation*: we can use 'all' to mean 'everything', but only in the form of 'all that'.

56   B   *Explanation*: 'hadn't hardly' and 'hadn't scarcely' both involve an unnecessary double negative. C is wrong because 'sale' is spelt 'sail'.

57   D   *Explanation*: we borrow something from someone and lend someone something; we say 'borrowed' something so that we could do something.

58 B *Explanation*: we say *at* hours (at 3 o'clock) *in* the afternoon/ evening, etc, *at* the weekend and *in* a month or year.

59 D *Explanation*: sarcasm uses mockery to convey contempt.

60 C *Explanation*: we use 'throughout' to say that something is in every part; 'it's' is the contraction of 'it is', while the possessive is 'its'.

61 A *Explanation*: we can use either 'you' or, rather formally, 'one'; however, we do not switch between them. In this example we cannot use 'you' as it is wrong to say 'you gets'.

62 B *Explanation*: the sentence requires everyone to help with finding both the culprit and the money, so 'everyone' must be placed where it applies generally.

63 C *Explanation*: 'kind' is singular and so requires agreement with 'trainer' rather than 'trainers', and it also requires the modifier 'this'.

64 A *Explanation*: when we refer to two objects we use 'between'; when there are more that two we use 'among'. To 'lie' is to recline, while to 'lay' is to lay something, so involving a reference to something, in this case the sheets.

65 D *Explanation*: we use the structure 'neither ... nor' when there is a common position and in this case the verb matches the noun that precedes it.

66 B *Explanation*: when we construct a sentence with 'either/or' we place the correlatives as close as possible to the subject to which they refer.

67 D *Explanation*: 'papers' are plural and so require the plural verb, while the request for the newspaper cuttings was singular, so it requires the singular verb.

68 A *Explanation*: 'trade federation' is a singular subject, so takes the singular 'has' rather than the plural 'have', and it is not a person, so we use 'its' rather than 'their'.

69 D *Explanation*: we can infer that there is a class of people who had previously challenged the chief executive and therefore in its correct form the sentence needs the demonstrative pronoun 'from those'.

70 C *Explanation*: the subject of the sentence 'is' a singular fact and so carries a singular verb, 'proves'.

71   A   *Explanation*: suggested answers B and D do not make sense. The form of the sentence is the past conditional and it therefore requires the past perfect conditional, 'had not taken'.

72   B   *Explanation*: the causal link between the two fragments of the sentence leads us from the first to the second, so we use 'so' to make the link rather than the alternatives. Were the link the other way around then we would use 'because'.

73   A   *Explanation*: the sentence is in the past conditional, so needs the past perfect conditional clause.

74   D   *Explanation*: note that 'too' can mean in addition, like, also, as well and not very. We construct sentences usually with 'also' in mid position, while 'too' and 'as well' usually occur at the end of a clause. We would not correctly say the food was 'too well cooked'. We would not say something was 'too ... as well'.

75   D   *Explanation*: 'number' refers to countable items, 'amount' refers to uncountable quantities. When making a comparison we say 'as ... as' and not 'as ... that'.

76   C   *Explanation*: something is either impossible or not and we avoid saying 'very impossible' or 'fairly impossible', but we do say 'quite impossible' for emphasis.

77   C   *Explanation*: an expression is a personification when human attributes are assigned to non-human things. In C money is said to talk, which is a personification.

78   D   *Explanation*: we use the same structure when constructing a sentence, so it is correct to say 'check' and 'double-check' or 'checking' and 'double-checking', but not to mix the structures. The correct verb tense for the sentence is determined by 'they had', which makes 'was time' correct.

79   A   *Explanation*: 'alternate' means 'every other', while 'alternative' means 'another'. 'All together' means 'everyone', while 'altogether' means 'completely'.

80   B   *Explanation*: the friend is a new one, so it is better to say that you made a new acquaintance.

81   D   *Explanation*: we say 'bread and butter', 'knife and fork' and 'hands and knees', and it is considered wrong to change the order. It is correct to say either 'you try to eat' or 'try and eat'.

82 C *Explanation*: 'affect' means influence, while 'effect' means cause, and in this case it is an influence affecting the resolve of the committee members, who are people, so referred to as 'their' rather than an object referred to as 'its'.

83 A *Explanation*: hyperbole is a description that is an over-exaggeration, and to say that someone would 'give the Earth' is an exaggeration as no one has the Earth to give.

84 D *Explanation*: a train moves *along* or *on* a track and passengers jump *off on to* the station platform.

85 B *Explanation*: to be cynical involves expressing the view that people are motivated by self-interest alone, and answer B most closely reflects this sentiment.

86 C *Explanation*: we do not start a sentence with 'Not any' but say 'No' instead; 'some expert' could be an expert in any field, while to say 'any expert' means it does not matter which – they will all agree. We say either 'could turn up any time' or 'will turn up some time'; both expressions are correct in this context.

87 D *Explanation*: 'into' makes clearer the action mother suggested. A and C are incorrect because 'like' should not be used as a conjunction (although it often incorrectly is).

88 C *Explanation*: a euphemism is when we substitute a polite word for one that may seem offensive or insensitive, and we often substitute 'passing away' for 'died'.

89 A *Explanation*: 'through' means to make a hole, 'though' means 'despite the fact'; we can correctly structure the sentence as 'although it was...' or 'foggy as it was...' or 'foggy though it was...' but we cannot correctly use the structure 'foggy as though it was'.

90 B *Explanation*: 'datum' is singular ('data' is the plural), so it is correct to say 'is'. The sentence needs 'it is' or its abbreviation 'it's' to read correctly.

91 D *Explanation*: the subject is computers and the object the world. In D the verb 'to run' directly transmits from the subject to the object.

92 D *Explanation*: 'if' and 'would' cannot be placed together in the same clause; instead we use 'had'.

93 C *Explanation*: because the sentence starts with 'anyone' we say 'they' rather than 'you' or 'she'.

94 D *Explanation*: a simile involves drawing a comparison between two unlikely things and takes the form '...like' or 'as...'.

95 C *Explanation*: in this context 'hopefully' means full of hope, and before it could make sense the sentence would need to read '... that he was full of hope that his team...'.

96 D *Explanation*: we use 'at' when locating a precise position or group activity, but 'in' when the position is large like a town.

97 C *Explanation*: 'at first' introduces a contrast, while 'first' is used to introduce an initial subject. 'Beside' means at the side, while 'besides' means as well as.

98 C *Explanation*: a recidivist is a criminal who reoffends, so in the case of A and B it is unnecessary to describe the recidivist as criminal and as reoffending. C is correct because we say 'to try to' and not 'to try and'.

99 B *Explanation*: a non-sequitur is a phrase or clause that does not follow locally from the previous phrase or clause. In the case of B the clause about sending the public back to school does not follow from the lack of trust.

100 A *Explanation*: the sentence is in the past conditional tense, so needs the past perfect conditional clause.

Chapter 5. 100 True, false or cannot tell questions

1   False *Explanation*: the passage states, 'The next time an astronaut walks there' but the subject of this statement is not walking to the moon.

2   Cannot tell *Explanation*: the passage states that the station will be engaged in scientific research and that its most ambitious task will be a manned mission to Mars, but we are not told of the station's principal (most important) objective and without knowing the principal of the objective we cannot tell.

3   False   *Explanation*: one reason given in the passage for the preference of this location is dependent on this assumption but the conclusion is not wholly dependent on this assumption because another reason given is the near continuous sunlight useful for the generation of solar power.

4   True   *Explanation*: the passage states that outside the cities people have no alternative but to use their cars; if these areas were served by an affordable public transport system then there would be an alternative.

5   Cannot tell   *Explanation*: the passage states that they (the people who live outside the cities) already pay among the highest petrol duties in the world but it does not stay whether or not they pay the same or a higher rate than those who live in the cities.

6   True   *Explanation*: the statement that the well-off driver will be able to continue driving while other drivers will not does assume that the new tax is sufficiently high to deter less-well-off car users.

7   False   *Explanation*: the passage states that cholera and the other identified diseases cause a great many deaths but not that cholera is a water-borne disease.

8   False   *Explanation*: the passage states that they make a significant contribution towards public health and that in the *British Medical Journal* they were voted the greatest medical breakthrough.

9   False   *Explanation*: the second sentence states that water has always been the greatest vector of disease but not that it still is the greatest.

10   True   *Explanation*: this is the meaning of the term 'gravy train'. Don't be tempted to answer 'cannot tell' just because the passage does not provide a definition of the term. You are expected to know the meaning of the words and terms used in these passages.

11   False   *Explanation*: the committee's comments were directed towards the public sector, not the private sector.

12   Cannot tell   *Explanation*: the passage reports an expensive waste but it is not quantified.

13   False   *Explanation*: 'ambivalent' means unsure, but in the passage the author's attitude is confident and disapproving.

14   False   *Explanation*: the passage states that pre-packed foods are expensive.

15   True   *Explanation*: the author argues for fresh food prepared by ourselves and eaten together and against processed food eaten in a hurry; it is probable therefore that the author would agree with the fact stated in the question.

16   True   *Explanation*: an explanation is an explanatory statement and the ultimate sentence in the passage is suitably explained in the question.

17   Cannot tell   *Explanation*: while this is an observation that many of us would recognize, it is not a subject covered in the passage, so we must conclude that we cannot tell.

18   True   *Explanation*: this is a reasonable statement of the principal point made in the passage.

19   True   *Explanation*: it says in the passage that particles were found that are older than our sun, and therefore older than our solar system, and that they remain in deep space unchanged.

20   False   *Explanation*: the passage does not comment on whether or not scientists were startled, so we know this statement to be untrue. (Note: had the questions not referred to the passage and stated only that 'The findings startled scientists', then the answer would have been 'cannot tell'.)

21   True   *Explanation*: 'rebutted' means disproved and it is stated in the passage that scientists were able to use spectrometers and electron microscopes to identify the mineral and chemical compositions of the particles.

22   Cannot tell   *Explanation*: the passage makes no comment on the fears of parents.

23   Cannot tell   *Explanation*: the passage reports that boys spend more on sporting activities than girls, but it does not say whether or not there is a gender trend in food-related spending, so we cannot say if they devote a greater part of their non-food spending on this activity than girls.

24   True   *Explanation*: the passage states that children spent equal sums on mobile phones and charges, and activities and objects that could be classed as educational. Books can be classed as educational but they are not the only object that can be so classed and while the amount is equal to that spent on mobile phones the amount spent is not detailed.

25   False   *Explanation*: the passage uses the term 'trend' in reference to the increase in the number of workers paying the top rate of tax.

26   False   *Explanation*: the passage states that 1 million people now pay tax at the higher rate because of the link between increases in tax allowances and inflation. The remaining 2 million people now pay tax at the higher rate because wages have risen at a rate higher than general inflation.

27   True   *Explanation*: this is a reasonable summary of the cause of the trend described in the passage.

28   True   *Explanation*: the passage states that users of virtual communities freely share their own work and all our cultural outpourings should be free to share. From this it can be reasonably inferred that the author would agree with the statement made in the passage.

29   False   *Explanation*: the passage does in fact present an either/or scenario: either payment is extracted or cultural outpourings should be free to share. No balance between these two positions is considered.

30   False   *Explanation*: the term in the context of the passage means the right to be recognized and acknowledged as the author, not the father.

31   True   *Explanation*: the author identifies what he sees as failings in the status quo and in the last sentence states that the world 'needs mechanisms capable of protecting' it.

32   False   *Explanation*: there is no reference to a revolution or anything that could be described as one, so this cannot be inferred from the passage.

33   False   *Explanation*: this is a tough question. You do not need to know anything of liberal politics to answer this question and the question is not asking you to say whether or not the explanation of that tradition provided in the question is correct. You need simply take the description provided of that school and decide if the passage is consistent with it. The passage is arguing for the global community to be protected from the excesses of individual national interests, which is quite different from the view that it is the interests of the nation state that need protecting.

34 Cannot tell   *Explanation*: another tough question. You cannot establish from the passage if the author believes the decision will establish or undermine the green credentials of the Commission.

35 True   *Explanation*: again a tough question. It is clear that some members are split – at least the environmental and industrial commissioners. The question does not ask if the Commission is split, which we cannot tell from the passage.

36 True   *Explanation*: a tautology is the unnecessary repetition within a statement of the same thing. In one statement of the passage it is said 'that is lowered annually, year on year', which is a tautology.

37 True   *Explanation*: it is stated in the passage that 'the majority of people, including many teachers, do not have a sufficient grasp of the rules to realize that a mistake has been made' and from this we can infer that most people don't object to bad grammar as they would not realize it was bad and so could not object.

38 False   *Explanation*: you cannot infer this as it is clear from the passage that people who do not know the rules are perfectly capable of breaking them and producing written work that contains bad grammar.

39 Cannot tell   *Explanation*: the author refers to the irritation some feel, but no information is offered as to whether or not the author believes that grammar matters for reasons other than this.

40 False   *Explanation*: the passage was deliberately unclear, however it describes January and February as the two warmest months worldwide, but these are only winter months in the northern hemisphere.

41 False   *Explanation*: the passages states that there were only two exceptions and China was not one of them, so we can infer that China *did* experience record temperatures.

42 Cannot tell   *Explanation*: we are not provided with the figures, so we cannot establish how the findings might have changed.

43 True   *Explanation*: the statement made in the question can be established as true because the passage describes it as the Eurozone, the countries mentioned are European and the data are described as downbeat or in other words disappointing.

44 True   *Explanation*: the passage states that no one now expects one and that retail, housing and manufacturing have slowed or are in decline.

45 False   *Explanation*: you cannot conclude from the passage that a cut will be made soon. The passage states 'the talk is of cuts, but for the time being anyway it is probably too early to say when a cut might be made'.

46 Cannot tell   *Explanation*: the passage does not comment directly on the feelings of children not included in the scheme, nor can it be inferred from the content of the passage.

47 False   *Explanation*: the passage states that a teacher in every school will lead on the project and rely on their peers to identify children, not the children themselves.

48 False   *Explanation*: that gifted children may not always behave themselves was given as a reason why the scheme may not succeed in identifying the really gifted or talented child rather than as a justification for the initiative.

49 False   *Explanation*: the case made in the passage is that Scandinavia is an egalitarian delight and that Greek men are the least reconstructed in Europe. If it were discovered that women want equality at home and for men to share domestic chores, then this would in fact support the case made in the passage, not weaken it.

50 False   *Explanation*: the purpose is to report the findings of a survey into who carries out domestic chores across Europe.

51 True   *Explanation*: it is possible that the statement is true.

52 Cannot tell   *Explanation*: the passage does not identify the beneficial forms of exercise. Where it is possible to infer that the researchers have identified the form of beneficial exercise from the passage it is not stated in the passage that they have.

53   False   *Explanation*: we cannot identify for whom the passage was written but we can conclude that it was not intended more for the group of physically inactive people over the population in general.

54   True   *Explanation*: the phrase 'is held to be' allows for other views and so for the possibility of disagreement.

55   True   *Explanation*: the passage states that four of the best five schools are US-based and the European Glasgow School is the only non-US school.

56   Cannot tell   *Explanation*: from the passage we know Lynx came first, Stanford second and Harvard third, but we do not know if Glasgow was in fourth or fifth place, only that it was the only non-US school in the top five.

57   Cannot tell   *Explanation*: neither the criteria nor the mechanism for grading the schools is commented on in the passage.

58   False   *Explanation*: the passage offers two possible explanations for the increase: one is that more young children develop the condition, the other is that the increase is due to a marked improvement in diagnosis. The second of these reasons, if correct, does not support the conclusion that five times as many young people are developing the condition. The same number of children would have developed the illness but few would have been diagnosed.

59   False   *Explanation*: the passage allows for two possibilities if the cause is environmental. One is something new that is the cause, the other is that we have reduced exposure to something that was previously providing protection.

60   True   *Explanation*: this is a reasonable explanation of the increase in cases.

61   True   *Explanation*: this fact would weaken the case made in the passage because it is claimed that mosquitoes in Italy are associated with every type of water body.

62   True   *Explanation*: 'genera' is the plural form of 'genus'; you can tell this from the passage because the passage states there are six genera of mosquitoes.

63   False   *Explanation*: no information is provided on this point in the passage.

64 Cannot tell   *Explanation*: the passage states that the atlas includes the earliest known printed plan of a US city but it does not say if the illustrations of England and Wales are the first or in the form of maps.

65 False   *Explanation*: the term 'attributed' means that an object is regarded as 'belonging or appropriate to' a person's work.

66 True   *Explanation*: 'multifunctional' means that something fulfils several functions and the passage states that the atlas provides an illustration of a survey of England and Wales and the expedition of Sir Francis Drake to the West Indies and what is now the United States.

67 True   *Explanation*: the passage states that the system ranks substances according to the harm they cause, for example the cost to the state. It is reasonable therefore to conclude that a drug's rating reflects its prevalence.

68 False   *Explanation*: this is a subsidiary point; the main point is that alcohol and tobacco cause more harm than many illegal drugs.

69 True   *Explanation*: the passage states that cannabis is below alcohol and tobacco in the league and that tobacco is ranked tenth. From this we can infer that cannabis is placed in the lower half.

70 True   *Explanation*: the passage states that the information will include details of the parents' education.

71 False   *Explanation*: we cannot infer from the passage that only middle class applicants will be required to disclose. If this were true then the wealthy person who retired early would not need to disclose anything.

72 False   *Explanation*: 'veracity' means in this context accuracy and other synonyms including truthfulness and honesty.

73 True   *Explanation*: 'duped' means misled and the author does suggest that consumers are misled into believing that the meat is British when the packaging shows the British countryside and the content is called 'farmhouse'.

74 Cannot tell   *Explanation*: to judge the statement as either true or false we would need more information regarding what constitutes a treatment or process resulting in a substantial change.

75   False   *Explanation*: the passage leads the reader to the view that the labelling of food as a product of the country in which the processing took place should be stopped, not the processing itself.

76   False   *Explanation*: they would pay the highest band of charge on public transport too.

77   False   *Explanation*: the passage makes no reference to the length of the journeys and so it cannot be inferred that the charge would depend on the length as well as the time of the journey.

78   False   *Explanation*: the question highlights a valid flaw in the comparison but the flaw has no bearing on the effectiveness of the charge in terms of its impact on congestion at peak times.

79   False   *Explanation*: strictly speaking, you might answer true to this question, but these questions are about judgement and it must be judged that the author did not literally mean 60 per cent of all the world's population, so the correct answer is false.

80   True   *Explanation*: by using the examples of the iPod and Nokia phone the author of the passage does focus on highly successful examples.

81   True   *Explanation*: the passage is making the point that successful brands go deeper than a catchy name and memorable logo and include the shape, feel and sound.

82   Cannot tell   *Explanation*: the passage does not provide information about the proportion of global economic activity that the United States enjoys now or 30 years ago. It only says that the US economy does not have the same clout or influence as it used to have; it could be the same size.

83   True   *Explanation*: the Europeans would have looked across the Atlantic and the Japanese across the Pacific when the adage that when the United States sneezes the rest of the world catches a cold was true.

84   False   *Explanation*: evidence in support of the hypothesis that when the United States sneezes the rest of the world no longer catches a cold would not show a link between a US recession and a downturn in the rest of the world.

85 False *Explanation*: in the passage the weather last week is described as balmy, ending in a cold snap. 'Balmy' means mild, so the week was mild but ended cold.

86 False *Explanation*: it is true that you cannot tell if it snowed this March but you cannot infer from the passage if snow in March is unusual. The passage states that March can bring snow or warm weather.

87 Cannot tell *Explanation*: the passage does not say if the flowers were early or not and we can't infer whether they were from the passage either.

88 Cannot tell *Explanation*: that hydroelectric schemes in temperate regions are less polluting may be the consequence of a number of causes and the passage does not provide an explanation.

89 True *Explanation*: the passage reports that the United Nations wants experts to examine the emissions produced by existing schemes and to recommend ways in which they can be made more environmentally friendly before more are built. It is reasonable to infer therefore that the United Nations does not think hydroelectric power is always a greener power source than alternatives and the passage tells you that hydroelectric power plants can be more polluting in the first few years.

90 Cannot tell *Explanation*: there is not sufficient information provided in the passage to confirm the truth or falsehood of the claim in the statement that methane is the greenhouse gas responsible for the emissions.

91 False *Explanation*: the passage states that the law will mean that all public bodies will have new responsibilities; by this it is meant governments and organizations providing services paid for from public funds, and a supermarket is not a public body.

92 False *Explanation*: a tough question. In respect of public services, while it is true that men and women often have different needs it cannot be inferred from the passage that this is the reason for the different experience men and women have of a service provided under a gender-neutral policy. It may be, for example, that the policy, while seemingly neutral, is not.

93 False   *Explanation*: this is a subordinate idea of the passage; the main one is that men and women should be treated equally.

94 True   *Explanation*: this is a valid summary of the author's intention.

95 False   *Explanation*: another tough question. An implied definition of 'spam' as unsolicited might be inferred from the passage but this is not a subordinate idea offered in the passage. An example of a subordinate idea from the passage would be the amount of spam doubling to the point where 19 out of 20 e-mails were unsolicited.

96 True   *Explanation*: the term used in the passage was 'seemed incredible', which means hard to believe. The passage states that 19 out of 20 e-mails were unsolicited, so this means only one in 20 were solicited, which is 5 per cent. Sorry to introduce maths, but verbal reasoning routinely involves the valid restatement or summary of numerical data. In business pretty much every e-mail, report or presentation will make reference to numerical data and will be judged better for it. So don't be surprised if some occurs at the periphery of a verbal reasoning test.

97 Cannot tell   *Explanation*: the outcome of the study is not reported in the passage and cannot be inferred from it.

98 False   *Explanation*: from the passage you can infer that the study is authoritative, definitive even, but we cannot infer from the passage if it is the most authoritative in the sense of the best study yet. Other studies may have been as authoritative or carried greater authority in respect of the reputation of the authors or some other feature.

99 True   *Explanation*: the passage states that mobile phones were introduced 20 years ago and fears of a link between their use and cancer have persisted throughout that period. It also states that the extent and duration of the new study means we can have great confidence in the result.

100 False   *Explanation*: the occurrence of more than 15,000 tumours would imply a link between using mobiles and the risk of cancer, but it would not weaken the conclusion of the passage because the passage does not comment on whether or not a link exists.

Chapter 6. Decision analysis

Decision analysis questions

1   C   *Explanation*: the code reads vote, must, turn around rich, turn around wrong. Turn around rich to get poor and turn around wrong to get right. Only suggested answers A and C make use of the full sequence but A is inconsistent with the context which states that the group champions the disenfranchised.

2   A   *Explanation*: the code reads equivalent merit, children, better, education. The equivalent to merit could be deserve, value or worth. Only A fully applies the sequence of code.

3   D   *Explanation*: the code reads must, high, accept, rich. Suggested answers A, C and D correctly apply the sequence of code but only answer D is consistent with the context. C is wrong because the context states that the group campaigns peacefully for its aims. A is wrong because the reason the rich must accept higher taxation is given (the redistribution of wealth).

4   C   *Explanation*: the code reads industry, must, pollution, similar reform, similar turn around high. Words similar to reform are modernized and transformation. Turn around high gives you low and words similar to low include, for example, lower. Only C correctly applies all parts of the sequence.

5   A   *Explanation*: the code reads wrong, similar poverty, public, similar rich. Similar to poverty can be poor or squalor and similar to rich can be wealth and affluence. D can be rejected because it uses the term wronged rather than wrong. B can be rejected because the term shortages is not similar to poverty. C (and also B) can be rejected because it contradicts the spirit of the context.

6   A   *Explanation*: the code reads enlarge reform, decrease better, must. Enlarge reform means revolution and change but not civil disobedience. Decrease better can mean OK, reasonable, tolerable and all right. Suggested answers A and C comply fully with the sequence of code but C can be rejected because it goes beyond the peaceful aims stated in the context.

7   B   *Explanation*: the code reads poverty, pollution, turn around result. Result means consequence or effect and to turn it around means basis, cause or foundation. Suggested answers A, B and C comply with the sequence of code. The context does not suggest or support the suggestion that pollution or poverty is the cause or effect of one or the other so we can reject these suggested answers. This leaves suggested answer B as the better interpretation in that it is most consistent with the tone of the context.

8   D   *Explanation*: the code reads education, children, turn around wrong, similar better. Turn around wrong means right and similar better can mean superior and good (if it were equivalent good would be incorrect). Suggested answers A, B and C do not apply the code sequence correctly. A and C fail to use the code for turn around wrong. B uses the term child rather than children.

9   C   *Explanation*: the code reads rich, pollution, equivalent better, similar turn around high. Equivalents of better are improved and healthier. A word similar to the opposite (turned around) of high is lower. Only suggested answer C applies the code sequence correctly.

10   A   *Explanation*: the code reads rich, turn around rich, must, better. Turn around rich gives poor. Suggested answers A and D correctly apply all aspects of the code sequence but D is not in line with the spirit of the context. Suggested answers B and C both fail to implement the code sequence fully.

11   B and C   *Explanation*: the code reads similar must, poverty, accept. Words and phrases similar to must include ought to, should and obliged. Suggested answer A applies the code correctly but is inconsistent with the spirit of the context. Suggested answer D does not make use of the code for accept.

12   A, B and D   *Explanation*: the code reads children, wrong, education, turn around rich. Turn around rich to obtain poor, deprived or underprivileged. Suggested answers A, B and D all correctly apply the code sequence and are consistent with the context. Suggested answer C does not make use of the code for wrong.

13   B and C   *Explanation*: the code reads high, similar public, reform. Words similar to public include unrestricted, community and civic. Suggested answers B and C correctly apply the code sequence and are consistent with the context. Suggested answer A fails to use the code for high while suggested answer D does not include a term similar to public.

14   A, B, C and D   *Explanation*: the code reads equivalent merit, reform, industry. Terms that are equivalent to merit include plus points, advantages, great value and worth. All four suggested answers correctly apply the sequence of code and are consistent with the context.

15   B and D   *Explanation*: the code reads reform, industry, accept, pollution, similar vote. Suggested answer A does not make use of the code for accept. And suggested answer C uses the term vote rather than a term similar to vote.

Four decision analysis mini-tests

Mini-test 1

1   B   *Explanation*: the code reads buy, any, similar to price. Similar to price can mean worth, cost, consequence and outlay. We can reject suggested answer A because the code for buy is not used (and because the term price is used rather than a term similar to it). We can judge C as incorrect because the code for 'any' is not utilized. Both suggested answers B and D correctly implement the sequence of code but suggested answer D is not consistent with the context, which states that the auction is of a unique British stamp so we cannot buy any of them (there is only one).

2   A   *Explanation*: the code reads million, twenty, Smith, bid. Suggested answers A and D both correctly apply the sequence of code but answer D is inconsistent with the context as it implies that the auction has already taken place and the context states that you are preparing for it.

3   C and D   *Explanation*: the code reads similar to buy, investment, stamp. Terms similar to buy include acquired, bought
and purchase. Suggested answer A can be rejected because
it uses the term buy rather than a term that is similar. Suggested
answer B fails to use the code for investment. Both C and D
correctly apply the sequence of code and are consistent with
the context.

4   D   *Explanation*: the code reads twenty, years, expand million,
sold, stamp. Expand million to get millions or countless. We
can reject suggested answer B as it uses an item from the list
of terms 'collectors' that is not in the sequence of code. Suggested answer C can be rejected because we say '20 million
is' and not '20 millions are'. Both suggested answers A and D
correctly apply the sequence but A is inconsistent with the
context which describes the stamp as unique.

5   B   *Explanation*: the code reads feature, stamp, cheap at,
unique, reverse similar to small, price. Terms that are similar to
the reverse of small include eye-catching, striking, titanic and
conspicuous. Suggested answer A fails to use the code for
cheap at. Suggested answer D uses the term cheap whatever
rather than cheap at. Suggested answers B and C both
correctly apply the sequence of code but C refers to 'the price'
and this is inconsistent with the context from which we can
infer that the auction has not yet taken place so the price
paid is not yet known.

Mini-test 2

1   A and C   *Explanation*: the code reads admit, children, parents, assignments. Suggested answer B does not use the
code for admit and D uses a term that occurs in the dictionary
but is not in the sequence of code. Both suggested answers A
and C apply the code correctly and are both consistent with
the context.

2   B   *Explanation*: the code reads nothing like big, websites,
model, offer. Terms nothing like big are small and modest
(full-length is like big rather than nothing like it). Suggested

answer A does not use a term nothing like big. Answer C does not utilize the term website or model (and uses the term grade which is in the dictionary but not in the sequence of code). Suggested answer D does not utilize the code for offer.

3 D *Explanation*: the code reads students, like admit, easy, cheat. Terms that are like admit include declare, come clean, say and confess. Suggested answers B and C do not utilize the code for easy. Both suggested answers A and D apply the code correctly but suggested answer A contradicts the context which states that cheating is widespread.

4 C *Explanation*: the code reads nothing like students, students, help. We can take nothing like to mean the opposite and the opposite of students can be teachers (but not learners). Suggested answer B and D fail to utilize a term nothing like student. Both suggested answers A and C comply with the code sequence and both are consistent with the context so we must decide which of the two in our judgement is best. Suggested answer C is the more relevant to the main issue of the context (also suggested answer A is to some extent implausible as it is not often you hear students complaining that they get too much help).

5 A *Explanation*: the code reads siblings, help, grade, parents, like increase. In the context a term like increase can be higher, boost, and inflation. Suggested answer D is nonsensical – we cannot correctly say that we can enlarge grades – and so can be rejected. Suggested answer B is questionable because it uses the term helped rather than help. Suggested answer B can also be rejected, along with answer C, because it is unclear what relevance it has to the context. Parents and siblings obviously can help students boost their grade through perfectly legitimate assistance. The point of the context is that grades may be boosted by parents and siblings helping in ways that amount to cheating. We can reject answers B and C, therefore, because parents and siblings can legitimately help students and this help can result in higher grades. This leaves answer A which complies with the code sequence and is consistent with the context.

Mini-test 3

1 C *Explanation*: the code reads treasure, join wood rock, similar to me. A term similar to me can be my, I, and mine. By joining wood and rock we can get coal and arguably a wooden box covered with rock. Suggested answer A can be rejected because even if we accept that joining wood and rock could give a rocky outcrop above the tree line, the context described the billionaire as an agoraphobic (someone fearful of open spaces) and we can suppose that he would not venture out onto such an exposed location. Suggested answer B does not make use of the code for a term similar to me. D uses a term (dig) that occurs in the lexis but is not included in the sequence of code.

2 D *Explanation*: the code reads stop, three, type of card game. The only types of card game in the suggested answers are bridge and poker. We can reject suggested answer A because a casino is not a type of card game. We can reject suggested answer B because the code is supposed to be directions to the treasure and three men could not be permanently playing a game of cards (the context states that he confided in no one so they could not be accomplices). We can reject suggested answer C because the context described the man as severely moral and we can surmise that such a person would not oblige another to play a game of poker.

3 B and D *Explanation*: the code reads rock, look, equivalent to flat. Terms that are equivalent to flat include smooth and apartment. We can reject suggested answers A and C because they do not utilize a term equivalent to flat (C uses the term flat not an alternative). A uses the term top which is not an equivalent to flat.

4 B *Explanation*: the code reads similar to wood, similar to circle, equivalent to broken rock. All the suggested answers include a term similar to wood; wooden, planks, tree and timber. Suggested answers A and D do not include a term similar to circle. Only suggested answer B contains a term that is the equivalent to broken rock, namely stones. In the context we are told that the treasure was buried and so if suggested answers A and C are referring to the location of the treasure then they both contradict the context.

5   A   *Explanation*: the code reads turn around mountain, join primitive plant cow, city. We can turn around mountain to get plane or valley and while only suggested answers B and C include the code for city by joining the primitive plant moss and cow we get the name of the city Moscow in suggested answer A (we can surmise that the set of street maps to most of the world's capital cities includes the city of Moscow which would allow us to identify it as a city). We can question B and D because in the case of B a hilltop and in the case of D a flat patch are not terms that mean the opposite of mountain and in neither is the code for 'turn around primitive plant cow' utilized. In C rainforest is not a primitive plant and again the code for join primitive plant and cow is not utilized. Given that we can identify Moscow as a city from the set of street maps the best answer is A.

Mini-test 4

1   D   *Explanation*: the code reads flight, nose, stable. All four suggested answers comply with the sequence of code so we must rely on the context to decide which is in our judgement the best. The context states that 'The ultimate design' involves 'a snub nose.' From this we can conclude that a snub nose is better than a pointed nose design and blunt is another word for snub. We can dismiss suggested answers A and C on the grounds that they described pointed nose designs as the better and we can identify D as the best interpretation because it states that a blunt nose is better and then goes on to explain why this is the case.

2   A and B   *Explanation*: the code reads design, construct, akin to choice. Terms that are akin to choice include best, choose and select. Suggested answer C does not include a term akin to choice and uses a term that occurs in the vocabulary but is not in the question's sequence of code. Suggested answer D

includes the terms delta and wing which are not in the question's sequence of code. Both A and B correctly apply the sequence and both are consistent with the context.

3 C *Explanation*: the code reads folds, tape, strength, minimize, drag. Suggested answer B uses the word design which occurs in the vocabulary but the code is not present in the sequence. Suggested answer D does not utilize the term tape. Both suggested answers A and C correctly apply the sequence of code but answer A contradicts the context which states that the use of tape is not allowed.

4 A and C *Explanation*: the code reads akin to slant, lift, increase, wing or wings, upwards. Terms that are akin to slant include incline and camber. Suggested answer B does not include a term akin to slant. Suggested answer D fails to include a word for upwards. Both A and C utilize all parts of the sequence and do not contradict the context.

5 B *Explanation*: the code reads expand important, design, wing or wings, nose. Expand important to get fundamental and vital (significant and central are equivalents to important rather than an expansion of it). Suggested answer A uses a term that occurs in the vocabulary but is not in the code sequence. Suggested answers C and D use equivalents to important rather than an expansion. Also, D is in conflict with the context which describes both the nose and wing as key.

Chapter 7. Four timed realistic tests with interpretations of your score

Test 1. Sentence sequence

1	DACB	2	BDAC	3	BDAC
4	DCBA	5	CBDA	6	BDCA
7	CBAD	8	DCAB	9	CBDA
10	BDCA	11	CADB	12	BADC
13	ADCB	14	BADC	15	CBAD

16	DBCA	17	CDBA	18	BADC
19	CADB	20	DBCA	21	CABD
22	ABCD	23	DABC	24	CBDA
25	BCDA	26	DACB	27	CADB
28	BDAC	29	DBCA	30	CBDA
31	DCBA	32	BADC	33	CADB
34	ACDB	35	ADCB	36	ABDC
37	CBAD	38	DCAB	39	ABCD
40	BADC				

Test 2. Word swap

1   she and who
2   substances and vegetables
3   drink and drinks
4   residues and pesticides (you cannot stop using residues)
5   component and per cent
6   (first) beautiful and intended
7   Poles and immigrants
8   bay and acres
9   elsewhere and will
10 implement and develop
11 (first) in and between
12 when and it
13 pulses and lentils
14 wet and warm
15 and and between
16 only and both
17 discovered and confirmed
18 two and one
19 were and was
20 conventional and hybrid
21 evolutionary and important
22 refinement and combination
23 (first) business and cashflow
24 management and successful
25 death and stroke

26 valuable and record
27 carrying and sent
28 would and said
29 disasters and earthquakes
30 leave and moving
31 achievements and research
32 law and justice
33 held and campaigned
34 nurture and talent
35 were and where
36 (first) many and few
37 figures and citizens
38 their and (second) that
39 seemed and seem
40 inevitable and (third) a

Test 3. English usage

1   D   *Explanation*: we say 'loudly' to mean a noise and 'aloud' when something is spoken rather than read without speaking. B does not make sense.

2   A   *Explanation*: 'because of' is wrong in B but correct in the structure used in D. Answer A is correct because when counting back in time we say 'ago' and not 'before'.

3   D   *Explanation*: an oxymoron occurs when two words have opposite meanings (kindness and suffocating) but when used together they make sense.

4   B   *Explanation*: 'permitted' is more formal but otherwise means the same as 'let' and 'allowed', but in this case the sentence is constructed in the passive form, which is formal, so the correct answer is 'permitted'.

5   B   *Explanation*: the marriage of 20 years continues from the past until the future (next Wednesday) so the future perfect tense 'will have been' is correct.

6   D   *Explanation*: we can say 'pretty well', 'nearly', 'almost', 'very nearly' and 'practically', but not 'very almost', 'pretty well almost' or 'nearly practically'.

7   A   *Explanation*: we only say 'over' and 'below' when something is literally over or under another thing, otherwise we say 'above' or 'below'.

8   B   *Explanation*: we would say 'didn't' if we had something to do but did not do it, and 'mustn't' if something was not allowed. Because the announcement did not occur until after the work was done we can infer that they did work over the weekend and if we do something that was not necessary we say 'needn't'.

9   D   *Explanation*: 'or else' means 'otherwise', 'all else' means 'all other'. 'Effective' means it works, while 'efficient' means no effort is wasted.

10   B   *Explanation*: expressing irony involves saying the opposite to what is intended or expected. If he was really not hungry, then you would not expect him to order so much food.

11   D   *Explanation*: 'loose' means movable, 'lose' means misplace. We say 'to' something rather than 'till'.

12   C   *Explanation*: always mention the other person or persons first and leave yourself last. Put the completed action first and the second action in the past tense.

13   C   *Explanation*: we say that we play or stand *in* the rain, not *under* it.

14   B   *Explanation*: when making a comparison avoid mixing infinitive and finite forms of verbs.

15   A   *Explanation*: 'a few' means 'some', while 'few' means 'not many'; likewise 'a little' and 'little' mean 'some' and 'few' but are correctly used when referring to uncountable nouns.

16   D   *Explanation*: to refuse is to not take something offered, to deny is to answer in the negative. A proposition should properly follow the direct object.

17   A   *Explanation*: when the main clause is in the past tense we use 'would'.

18   A   *Explanation*: we use the present simple tense when describing something we do. D is incorrect because it does not make sense.

19   C   *Explanation*: 'shadow' refers to shade of a particular shape, while we use 'middle' rather than 'centre' if we are not suggesting accuracy.

20   D   *Explanation*: the information about dog breeds is irrelevant to the question, which is investigating the misuse of two negatives. Two negatives should be avoided as they change the sense to affirmative, so A and B are grammatically incorrect. C does not make sense.

21   B   *Explanation*: when an event is happening at the time of speaking we use the present continuous: enjoying, doing, etc.

22   B   *Explanation*: 'price' is that paid by the customer, while 'cost' is the amount paid at wholesale.

23   D   *Explanation*: when we refer to a period that continues to the present we use the present perfect: 'travelled', 'been', 'visited'.

24   A   *Explanation*: you can die *of* hunger but not *from* hunger. You can die *of* or *from* the wounds received *in* but not *by* battle.

25   C   *Explanation*: 'do' and 'does' are the present simple tense, which we use to talk in general about things that happen all the time. We use 'do' when we refer to ourselves, you and they, and 'does' for the third person and for inanimate objects: we, he, she or it.

26   D   *Explanation*: we can correctly say either 'tell me' or 'say', but we must identify the subject in both cases as they are different.

27   B   *Explanation*: the deal is still not closed, so we say 'have been'.

28   A   *Explanation*: we use 'keep' or 'kept' when referring to something permanent, and 'made of' when the material is identifiable. We would prefer 'made from' when, for example, the process of manufacture made it impossible to identify the material.

29   B   *Explanation*: both 'scissors' and 'pair of scissors' are correct, but we don't use the singular 'scissor' (we often use 'pair' when referring to things made from two parts). The plural of 'child' is the irregular 'children'.

30   A   *Explanation*: 'do you like' means 'do you enjoy something'; 'do you want' enquires into your wishes, 'would want' or 'would like' are more polite but it does not make sense as phrased in the other suggested answers.

31 D *Explanation*: 'at present' means 'now', while 'presently' means 'soon'. It is incorrect to say *before* two weeks; we would say two weeks *ago*.

32 C *Explanation*: use 'many' for plural nouns and 'much' for uncountable nouns.

33 B *Explanation*: we use 'elder' when referring to people, especially relatives, but not if followed by the word 'than'.

34 D *Explanation*: we could say 'too bitter' or 'very bitter' but not 'much bitter' ('very' would be used for emphasis). We use 'each' when referring to the individual and 'every' to a group.

35 A *Explanation*: the original came first so it is different *to* not *from* the sequel. 'Than' is a conjunction, so is incorrect when making a comparison. The film would be guilty *of* not *for*.

36 C *Explanation*: we use the present continuous – rising, doing, working, etc – when we refer to something happening at the time of speaking or writing.

37 C *Explanation*: we correctly say either 'visits to' or 'visiting'. 'Kind' is singular, so this must agree with 'this' rather than 'these'.

38 A *Explanation*: 'all' meaning 'everybody' takes a plural verb, while 'all' meaning 'everything' takes a singular verb.

39 B *Explanation*: we would correctly say 'afterwards' and use the adjective 'open', not the past participle 'opened'.

40 D *Explanation*: we do not use the present continuous tense in the case of 'thinking' (it is not an action like doing); instead we use the present continuous 'think'.

Test 4. Reading comprehension and critical reasoning

1 False *Explanation*: it cannot be inferred that trace levels of Acrylamide are toxic. The levels at which the animal studies found it to be a carcinogen are not stated nor can they be inferred. The passage states that an urgent search began to establish the risk and this suggests that the extent to which trace levels might prove toxic are unknown.

2   Cannot tell *Explanation*: we are told that it was 2002 when news of the presence of Acrylamide in many foodstuffs emerged and the passage states that an urgent search had begun, but the date that the passage was written is not known nor are we given an indication of the timescale in which answers might be found. For these reasons it cannot be known if the author would disagree (or agree) with the view that answers to the questions raised about the safety of Acrylamide should by now be close to being found.

3   False *Explanation*: the issue of how difficult it might prove to remove the substance from the human food chain has no bearing on the likelihood that the ingestion of Acrylamide poses a health risk.

4   Cannot tell *Explanation*: it is not stated in the passage whether or not Britain will realize its Kyoto target, nor can this information be inferred from the passage.

5   False *Explanation*: the passage does not state this, but that emissions would be lower if more radical policies had been adopted can be inferred from the passage. But the question does not ask what can be *inferred* from the passage, only what is *stated* in the passage.

6   True *Explanation*: the passage starts with the announcement of 1997 and the progress made towards the target until 2002; it then considers the setback after 2002 and the admission of failure to realize the target in 2005. Thus it is true to say that the passage follows events chronologically.

7   True *Explanation*: it is stated in the passage that political parties should vote to increase taxpayers' support; it can be inferred from this that there is already a state subsidy paid.

8   False *Explanation*: the second sentence of the passage states the details of the compromise, not the stand-off.

9   True *Explanation*: reference is made in the details of the compromise to the cap or ceiling to donations, but it is not suggested or inferred that agreement has been reached over this point. Equally there is nothing in the passage that suggests the parties may not remain divided over the issue of spending limits on both local and national elections.

10   True   *Explanation*: the passage states that Yulia Tymoshenko split from the 'Our Ukraine Party' to run her own election campaign.

11   True   *Explanation*: while it is clear from the passage that 'The Party of Regions' received the highest percentage of votes, the passage states that 'the result means that the next government of the Ukraine is likely to be a coalition' and from this we can infer that the election failed to produce an outright winner.

12   Cannot tell   *Explanation*: the passage states that Tymoshenko was sacked from a ministerial post and split from the 'Our Ukraine Party' and it also states that the President and leader of the 'Our Ukraine Party' is Mr Yushchenko, but it cannot be inferred from this that is was necessarily Mr Yushchenko who sacked Ms Tymoshenko.

13   True   *Explanation*: an ambidextrous person is able to use right and left hands equally well. The passage describes the ambidextrous dogs as showing no preference for left or right.

14   False   *Explanation*: the case made in the passage would be greatly *weakened* if this characteristic was manifest before the dogs began training as there would be no need for a new test.

15   True   *Explanation*: such a test would be of commercial interest because it could reduce the number of dogs that start training but are later found to develop this undesirable characteristic.

16   False   *Explanation*: the main theme (point) of the passage is to describe how the planned closure of 2,500 rural post offices will greatly worsen rural isolation.

17   True   *Explanation*: the passage opens with a definition of rural isolation as a lack of access to essential economic and social components and then goes on to illustrate that isolation with examples from public transport and access to shops and government services.

18   Cannot tell   *Explanation*: the author is likely to agree that there is a risk of this occurring, but we cannot tell if the author would agree that a community shop would close if the post office based in it is closed.

19   False   *Explanation*: the passage states that animals in the tropics exhibit fewer seasonal variations in behaviour and therefore it is not true to say that *all* animals dramatically adapt their behaviour to suit the seasons.

20   False   *Explanation*: the passage does not provide an explanation as to why tropical animals' behaviour is less sensitive to the season.

21   True   *Explanation*: the author refers to shift-workers and long-distance flyers generally as well as most workers and children in northern latitudes.

22   Cannot tell   *Explanation*: the passage does not provide any detail of the environmentalists' campaign against the 4×4 and so we are unable to tell if the research findings would undermine that campaign.

23   False   *Explanation*: the passage states that people were put off by the high running costs of these vehicles, suggesting that the passage is based on the assumption that 4×4s are fuel inefficient, but the passage is not based on any assumption regarding the relative inefficiency of these cases compared with older types of car.

24   True   *Explanation*: it is stated in the passage that existing owners face significant losses should they decide to sell, and from this we can deduce that second-hand values have dropped significantly.

25   False   *Explanation*: a tough question. The passage does not state that it was a surprise that the number of new cases should fall but that the rate and speed of the fall was a surprise.

26   True   *Explanation*: it would be wrong because the rise in cases over two decades is attributed to two factors – the aging population and screening – and we do not know which effect was responsible for the increase of new cases at which time.

27   True   *Explanation*: 'contingent' means true by the way things are rather than logically true, and the passage describes a factual association between the fall in cases and the decrease in the number of women taking the therapy.

28   True   *Explanation*: this is a valid restatement of the opening sentences. The forbear who believed the moon was really the size it appears in the sky would not want to create the impression of depth for his picture to be representational.

29 False *Explanation*: another tough question. While we can infer that the ancient Egyptians did not share our need to create the illusion of depth in their paintings, this does not allow us to conclude that they never created the illusion in their perspective in the art.

30 True *Explanation*: the example given describes two methods; 'if parallel lines are shown to converge' and objects 'at a distance are depicted as smaller'.

31 False *Explanation*: the author *would* agree with this statement as it is consistent with the statement made in the passage that the citizens of these countries hold 90 per cent of the world's wealth.

32 False *Explanation*: the passage does not make the assumption that the world's poor live in certain countries as it acknowledges that within the countries that make up the wealth zones there is inequality between rich and poor.

33 Cannot tell *Explanation*: the passage does not comment on the risk of tension created by the inequity and whether or not such tension exists cannot be inferred either.

34 Cannot tell *Explanation*: the geographic location of the porcelain is not identified in the passage.

35 False *Explanation*: the passage does not provide details on the relative popularity of the white and later painted porcelain.

36 False *Explanation*: the passage describes the colour of the porcelain that utilized the newly discovered Persian cobalt as blue and white, not green.

37 False *Explanation*: a tough question. It is clear from the passage that the term 'serious crime' *includes* the offences of murder and attempted murder, but it is not possible to infer that the term can be defined to mean murder and attempted murder.

38 False *Explanation*: another tough question. The passage argues that serious crime is committed by criminals on probation because they are released early, not because they are inadequately supervised.

39   Cannot tell   *Explanation*: murder can happen in prison as well as when a person is under the supervision of the probation service, so we cannot know if 100 murders would have been avoided or not.

40   False   *Explanation*: a hundred years ago washing machines and running hot water would not have featured in a list of indicators of poverty.

41   True   *Explanation*: if the definition of poverty is set according to a middle (median) income value, then it is possible that the number of people who are classed as poor will increase if they do not keep up with the rate at which society's wealth increases.

42   True   *Explanation*: according to the passage this would be an acceptable definition of absolute poverty and people would not be poor in absolute terms if they are fed, clothed and housed.